ORDNANCE SURVEY
Touring Atlas
SCOTLAND

TEMPLE PRESS

Acknowledgements

The publishers are grateful to Ross Finlay, who provided material on which the Introduction and Area Guides are based, and to the following for photographs:

Photographic acknowledgements

Ken Andrew 22, 25, 30, 45, 51; Derek Forss 31; William Grant & Sons Ltd 20 top; Great Scot! Pictures, Edinburgh 4, 10; The Hamlyn Publishing Group Limited/Chris King 18 top; A. F. Kersting 20–1, 26, 27, 28, 36, 56–7; Trustees of the National Library of Scotland, Edinburgh 6–7; National Trust for Scotland, Edinburgh 15, 24; Nature Photographers Limited, Basingstoke: T. Andrewartha 46, M. R. Hill 12, David Hutton 38–9, Paul Sterry 42–3; The Photo Source, London 9, 11, 33, 34, 39, 44, 52; Scottish Tourist Board, Edinburgh 5, 14, 16, 17, 43, 48; Bob and Sheila Thomlinson 13, 18–19, 40, 47, 50, 53, 54; Judy Todd 32.

First published 1988 by

Ordnance Survey and	Temple Press, an imprint of
Romsey Road	The Hamlyn Publishing Group Limited
Maybush	a Division of The Octopus Publishing Group plc
Southampton	Michelin House, 81 Fulham Road
SO9 4DH	London SW3 6RB

Maps and Index Copyright © Crown Copyright 1988

Airport, Ferry port and Motorway Strip Maps Copyright © Ordnance Survey and The Hamlyn Publishing Group Limited 1987

Introduction and Area Guides Copyright © The Hamlyn Publishing Group Limited 1988

ISBN 0 600 55655 7
(Ordnance Survey ISBN 0 319 00148 2)

Printed in Italy

Contents

History

SCOTLAND HAD BEEN INHABITED for thousands of years before the people called the Scots – relative latecomers in the time scale of history – left Ireland around A.D. 500 to establish the little west-coast kingdom of Dalriada, from which their influence gradually extended over the whole country.

Much earlier, as the climate became warmer after the last Ice Age, there were settlements of primitive cave-dwellers, who left behind no buildings, in fact no structures of any kind – only sea-shells, flints and domestic debris, dated in one excavation near Oban to approximately 5000 B.C.

By about 3000 B.C., better-organized communities had developed. Orkney, in particular, has some of the finest Neolithic sites in Europe, such as the village of Skara Brae and the superb barrel-vaulted burial chamber at Maes Howe, built long before the pyramids of Egypt.

Another millennium later, all over the north and west of Scotland, rows and circles and individual examples of standing stones were erected. Some, like the great megalithic circle at Callanish in Lewis,

Monuments to two great Scots stand high above Stirling – to Robert the Bruce at the castle, and in the distance the 19th Century Wallace Monument is prominent on Abbey Craig

suggest that their builders were no strangers to detailed astronomical observations.

A few centuries after, hundreds of hilltop forts were built, providing both extensive views and natural defences which could be augmented by ditches, earth banks and palisades. Traprain Law in East Lothian and Eildon Hill North above Melrose were the sites of substantial towns.

The Celtic peoples who inhabited Scotland at the time of Christ comprised two basic groups. In the north were the Picts, although that name – from the Latin *Picti* (the 'painted ones') – was given to them later. In the south were the Britons, one of whose tribes had as its capital the place which became Edinburgh.

Accustomed to outside marauders, and indeed to attacks from closer neighbours too, they had never, before the arrival of the Romans, encountered anything like a properly disciplined, centrally organized, and well-equipped army. Julius Agricola was the first great Roman commander to campaign in Scotland. His men surveyed and built the road called Dere Street, whose course can still be traced as it sweeps down out of the Cheviot Hills, past the confusion of Roman camp sites at Pennymuir and on beyond the Eildon Hills to the port of Cramond on the Forth.

Then they established a series of forts of their own, along the low ground between the Forth and the Clyde, which were to be linked, after A.D. 140, by the most northerly defended line of the whole Roman Empire, the ditch-and-rampart Antonine Wall.

Although the period after the Roman withdrawal is called the Dark Ages, this is the time when the light of Christianity began to shine. St Ninian established a church at Whithorn in Galloway, traditionally in the year 397. In 563 St Columba brought Celtic Christianity from Ireland to the western island of Iona. It became the religion of the kingdom of Dalriada, which the Scots from Ireland centred on their hilltop fortress of Dunadd.

In the east the Picts had progressed well beyond their status as painted warriors whom the Romans had been unable to subdue. All over the territory they occupied there are even now lasting memorials to them in the form of graceful and intricately carved stones.

However, their days were numbered. In 839 the Danes annihilated a Pictish army and killed most of the ruling family. At the same time, the Scots in the west were coming under intense pressure from savage Norwegian raids. Kenneth MacAlpin, king of Dalriada, shrewdly judging the situation, moved into the Central Highlands, the heart of Pictland. There he ruled over a combined kingdom of the Scots and the surviving Picts, well away from the coasts and islands which were under constant Viking threat.

The Norman Conquest of England, which began in 1066, never extended, in terms of control of land, to Scotland, but Anglo-Norman influences did make their way northwards. Scottish kings conferred grants of land upon noble Norman families.

All this time, however, the Norsemen ruled the north and west mainland and the islands. It was not until 1263, during the reign of a strong Scottish king, Alexander III, that they were defeated at the Battle of Largs. Alexander's death, in a riding accident one stormy night in 1286 on the cliffs above Kinghorn in Fife, plunged the country into political chaos. His heiress was his infant grand-daughter Margaret, daughter of the King of Norway, but she died on her voyage across the North Sea.

Clans and tartans

The most notable feature of the social structure of the old Highlands and Islands was its division into clans – extended families, often numbering tens of thousands of people closely or remotely related, with the same surname as the chief of the clan, or the surname of one of its minor dependent families.

In the early days, though, there were no surnames. A man might be called the Gaelic equivalent of Allan, son of Donald. Now, he would be known as Allan MacDonald, or Allan Donaldson.

It is still a characteristic of Highland and especially Hebridean people that family trees are the subject of instant and detailed recall, when someone, rarely seen and perhaps living on the other side of the world, is accurately placed as the cousin of a brother-in-law of a particular aunt.

Major clan chiefs were people of great influence, able to call on the services of thousands of fighting men. The MacDonald Lords of the Isles – who traced their ancestry back to a fourth-century Irish prince, and from whom the present clan chief is descended – held sway over a huge 'sea kingdom' in the western mainland and many of the islands, and were able as virtually independent rulers to defy the wishes of the Scottish kings. The Lords of the Isles did not submit until the time of James IV in the 1490s.

The chiefs had substantial powers in territories which were often very extensive. Even in Victorian times the

The Tartans Museum at Comrie houses a fascinating collection of tartans and Highland Dress. Hand weaving demonstrations, together with spinning and dyeing, bring this most widely-known feature of Scotland to life at the museum

The 17th Century map of Scotland by John Speed. The figures in the corners show Highland Dress of the period

The Yles of Orknay

A Scale of Miles

SUTHERLAND

Stranavern

Caithnes

Dunesbe head

Rosse

Ardmanoth

MURAY

BUQUHAN

Aberdone

New Aberdone

Marria

Mernia

Athole

Broad
Albayn

Dunkell

Perth

THE GERMANE

SEA

Fife nes

Lac
Lomond

Sterling

Stineling

Lenox

LOUTHIANE

Edynburgh

Twedale

Douglas dale

Clides
dale

Kyle

Anandale

Liddisdale

Galloway

Carlile

PART OF

ENGLAND

A Scotch Woman

A Highland woman

Performed by John Speed and are
to be sold by Roger Rea y Elder &
younger at y Golden Crosse in
Cornhill against the Exchange

Alexander had kept the ambitions of his noblemen firmly in check. After the death of the 'Maid of Norway', as Margaret was called, all their rivalry came to the surface in a welter of conflicting claims to the throne. In a moment of collective madness they invited to act as arbitrator the one man in the whole of Europe who would benefit most from the choice of a weak, or at least a malleable, Scottish king – Edward I of England.

He declared in favour of John Balliol, who did indeed have a convincing claim to the throne, but proved to be, for most of his short reign, exactly the kind of weak-minded individual Edward desired. From the very beginning Balliol accepted the status of Edward's vassal.

Not everyone acquiesced in this virtual surrender. Sir William Wallace campaigned against the English occupation for several years, until he was shamefully betrayed to them and even more shamefully butchered at his execution in London.

In circumstances which at first seemed faintly ridiculous Wallace's example was unexpectedly taken up by another of the earlier claimants to the throne, Robert Bruce, Lord of Annandale and Carrick, and Edward's one-time courtier.

Bruce had himself crowned king of Scotland. After a seven-year struggle he won control over almost the whole country. The final confrontation came in 1314 when the English army, by then under the command of

Edward II, faced that of Bruce at Bannockburn near Stirling.

There, Robert Bruce, the former guerrilla leader, showed himself to be a master of both planning and morale. Bannockburn was an overwhelming victory for his heavily outnumbered army, and re-established Scotland's independence on the European scene.

A few years after Bruce's death in 1329, his son-in-law Robert II established the royal house of Stewart, now generally known as Stuart.

Wars with England continued intermittently, especially as Scotland was now linked in the 'Auld Alliance' with France. James IV was Henry VIII's brother-in-law, but in 1513, when Henry was warring with France, James responded to an appeal from King Louis and invaded England. At Flodden in Northumberland his army was wiped out by the brilliant tactics of the Earl of Surrey. James and many of Scotland's leading aristocrats were killed – 'the flowers of the forest' in an old Scottish lament.

His son James V, succeeding to the throne at the age of one, proved to be another fine king, to whom we owe many of the Renaissance splendours of Falkland Palace and Stirling Castle. When he died in 1542, his daughter, Mary Queen of Scots, succeeded him at the age of less than a week. One of the most fascinating personalities of her time, she still has her partisans and detractors, arguing about her place in history.

The Border counties of Scotland were ravaged in the

property of the Marquis of Breadalbane, head of only one branch of the great Clan Campbell, stretched from Taymouth Castle east of Loch Tay to the Slate Islands off the coast of Argyll – more than 400,000 acres (160,000 ha) in one unbroken sweep across Scotland.

However, the idea of clan territory as the property of the chiefly family is a comparatively recent one. The original position was that the chief held the land in trust for all the members of his clan, agreeing to support them in times of trouble, and being guaranteed their swords in battle in return.

The 'pacification' of the Highlands after the failure of the last Jacobite rising in 1746 was a determined attempt to obliterate the whole idea of loyalty to a smaller unit – loyalty to a clan rather than to the central government. The prohibitions on holding weapons or wearing any kind of clan tartan which would reinforce the old loyalties were stern to the point of brutality. Men all over the Highlands were compelled to take an oath forswearing guns, swords and any kind of Highland dress. If a man reneged on his promise, so the oath continued: 'May I be accursed in my undertakings, family and property. May I never see my wife or children or father, mother or relations. May I be killed in battle as a fugitive coward, and lie without Christian burial in a foreign land, far from the graves of my forefathers and kindred.'

There was another important aspect of the government's policy. It abolished the legal powers of the clan chiefs and encouraged some of them to enter London society. To pay for their new and expensive way of life, they and their successors had to sell off land or increase the rents they charged their now distant clansmen.

A terrible potato blight in the 1840s caused a famine in the West Highlands and Islands, where farming had remained primitive. It speeded up the process of emigration which had already started and was

encouraged by the actions of many landowners in evicting smallholders to make way for better-paying, sheep-farming tenants.

These are some of the reasons for the great dispersal of Highlanders and Islanders overseas, to North America, Australia, New Zealand and elsewhere. But in modern times the sentimental attachment of fourth- or fifth-generation American-Scots, Canadian-Scots and the rest has given rise to renewed enthusiasm – abroad, perhaps, more than at home – for clan history and connections, for Highland gatherings and games, for the wearing of tartan, and for visits to clan chiefs: at Inveraray for the Campbells, Armadale Castle for the MacDonalds, Dunvegan Castle for the MacLeods, Duart Castle for the MacLeans, and so on.

Although clan tartans were harshly proscribed after the defeat of the last Jacobite rising, the rule applied only to Highland men living in Britain. Weavers of tartans were able to survive by supplying women and children, Scots abroad and the Highland regiments which – as a recruiting scheme – were allowed to retain them. Thus, when the proscription was lifted in 1782, the biggest tartan-marketing firm, William Wilson and Sons, operating from the remarkably suitable location of Bannockburn, were able to add to their business rather than having to start from scratch.

When George IV made a state visit to Edinburgh in 1822, egged on by Sir Walter Scott to deck himself out in something like full Highland dress, and when, later in the century, Queen Victoria and Prince Albert showed great enthusiasm for all things Scottish at their Highland home at Balmoral, the tartan increased again in popularity.

The designs, however, presented something of a problem. During the years of partial prohibition, most of them had been forgotten. When full-scale production began again and specific clan tartans were requested, Wilsons often asked the chiefs for confirmation that

The late-Neolithic settlement of Skara Brae was buried as sand encroached, and survived as a remarkable record of Orkney life, c 1500 BC. It is near the Bay of Skaill

some pattern or other would be acceptable, or simply nominated one themselves.

A few tartans date back beyond that time, but the history of modern tartans, a much disputed subject, really began at this period. However, even the ones which are less than 200 years old now have a settled pedigree.

Tartan design, in responsible hands, is by no means a slapdash affair, but a strictly artistic arrangement of lines and checks and a repeating pattern – the 'sett'. There is nothing symbolic about the colours.

The Scottish Tartans Society, various clan associations and some of the individual weavers keep detailed records of the 1500 or so individual tartans known, and create or approve appropriate new designs. The design process is subtle and there are remarkable variations possible within what may appear superficially to be a limited choice.

One aspect rarely noticed by the layman is that altering the colours while keeping the identical pattern changes a tartan out of all recognition. The MacNab, the MacLachlan and the much more sombre Black Watch tartans look completely different, but they all have exactly the same sett. This is a trick worked by the old-style handloom weavers for whom it was much easier to alter the colours on their looms than to reset them for different patterns.

Clan society may now have a different meaning from the one it had a dozen generations ago. However, on formal occasions, with men dancing in full Highland evening dress and their partners in long, light-coloured frocks with tartan sashes pinned to one shoulder by a Celtic brooch, the effect is not simply an imitation of the fashions of a time long gone by; it is a style still vigorous and elegant today.

1540s by English attacks – known as the 'Rough Wooing' – by means of which Henry VIII tried to force the Scots to pledge Mary in marriage to his son, thus paving the way for a joint kingdom united under the Tudors. She was sent instead to France where she married the dauphin who became, briefly, Francis II. After his early death she returned home to Scotland as the Catholic monarch of a country in the throes of the Reformation. After a turbulent reign, and surrounded by courtiers whose interests were certainly not her own, she was forced to abdicate in favour of her son James, who was, in true Stuart style, still only a child.

Mary sought refuge with her cousin Elizabeth of England, but there was even worse trouble to come. Next in line of succession to Elizabeth, she was, in the opinion of some parties, the legitimate queen of England and a potential rallying-point for the disaffected English Catholics. After nearly 20 years' house arrest she was executed.

Ironically, when Elizabeth died in 1603, the next in line to her throne was Mary's son, James VI of Scotland, who added the title of James I of England. Only the crowns and not the parliaments of the two countries were linked. But James so contrived matters that the Scottish parliament could do little more than impotently approve the decrees he issued at his new court in London. This arrangement was enthusiastically continued by his son Charles I, who meddled in the affairs of the national Church in Scotland. He tried,

Some 15 miles west of Stornoway on Lewis, the Callanish stone circle is one of three groups of standing stones in a small area on Lewis

for instance, to force bishops appointed by the crown on a Church which was firmly Presbyterian and opposed to any kind of hierarchy. This aroused so much opposition that a National Covenant was signed, pledging loyalty to the king but totally rejecting his policies on religion.

There was fighting. Charles saw reason and was about to change his mind when the Civil War erupted in his English realm. It spilled over into Scotland, with much bloodshed on both sides. When Cromwell had Charles beheaded, the Scots were furious that in executing the person who to him was the king of England, he had also killed the king of Scotland. Their response was to crown Charles's son as Charles II of Scotland. This enraged Cromwell, who took an army into Scotland and put the country under his iron rule.

At the Restoration, Charles II, now at last king of England as well, unexpectedly reintroduced into Scotland the episcopal form of church government which even his imperious father had eventually recognized as a mistake. Congregations which refused to comply simply held their services out of doors.

In 1670 a very unwise Act of Parliament declared these outdoor services to be treasonable. Adopting the name of Covenanters, some Presbyterians and their now itinerant preachers retreated to hold their services on remote hillsides, where they were hunted down by dragoons. Many a Scottish churchyard still has the graves of its 'martyrs of the Covenant' carefully maintained.

The last great political convulsion came in 1707. Not without a certain amount of bribery and corruption, but nevertheless by a majority, the Scottish parliament agreed to merge itself with the English one: perhaps the only example in history of a free parliament voting itself into oblivion. The Treaty of Union stated that England and Scotland would become one state – Great Britain.

But many supporters of the house of Stuart were unhappy at the arrival of the Hanoverian kings. A Stuart claimant to the throne – yet another James, whose father had ruled, briefly and badly, as James VII

and II – lived in exile abroad. Taking their title from the Latin version of his name, his adherents were called Jacobites. In 1715 the first Jacobite rising failed. A smaller, Spanish-financed affair in 1719 was on such a limited scale that it came to be known as 'The Attempt'.

Later, James's son Charles Edward Stuart – Bonnie Prince Charlie – headed the far more serious Jacobite rising of 1745. This did not have the support of all Scots. Many Lowlanders, in particular, were opposed to the Stuarts, and there were Scottish soldiers in the government ranks, but it was not an exclusively Scottish affair either, because there were Jacobite sympathizers in England too. Essentially, though, and in the public mind, it was largely Highland in its manpower, style, exuberance, drama and – looking back over the years – atmosphere of romance.

Although the Jacobites reached as far south as Derby, a long retreat northwards followed. Finally, at Culloden Muir near Inverness they faced a better-armed force under George II's son, the Duke of Cumberland. In exactly the wrong kind of set-piece battle for a still fearsome Highland army, they suffered a crushing defeat.

In the aftermath, Cumberland's men swept through the Highlands in a deliberate, murderous rampage. However, despite the huge price put on his head, the Prince was never betrayed during months of disguise and flight. In September 1746, when he sailed back to exile from a lonely West Highland sea loch, history had finally done with the ill-fated house of Stuart.

Modern Scotland has innumerable memorials and much-visited locations associated with Wallace and Bruce, the Covenanters and the Jacobites. Many groups within the country keep their memories vividly alive.

The struggles in which they took part may be long in the past, but Scotland retains its own established Church, its own legal and educational systems, its own banknotes and its own enthusiasms. And its people, whether unionist or nationalist by political persuasion, are quite clear that it is a different *place* from England, that 'England' and 'Britain', however casually confused in conversation south of the border, are not by any means one and the same thing.

Landscape

LOOKED AT ON SEPARATE MAPS, the east and west coasts of Scotland might well be in completely different countries. Although it has major indentations such as the five great firths – Dornoch, Cromarty, Moray, Tay and Forth – the east coast is generally smooth in outline, almost entirely lacking in islands and offering uninterrupted views to the horizon, out across the vast expanse of the North Sea. The west coast, by contrast, is a riot of island groups, peninsulas, sea lochs, fjords, bays, river mouths and mountains rising steeply from the Atlantic.

Scotland has a bewildering variety of landscapes.

Major forces have acted on the land and have left their tell-tale signs: volcanoes, glaciers, geological fault lines and the receding ocean levels which created the raised beaches marking the stranded shorelines of thousands of years ago.

Volcanic action, of course, came first. The granite peaks of Arran and the rough, dependable gabbro rocks of Skye – providing not just spectacular skyline ridges but also perfect rock-climbers' holds – are the

The Bass Rock, very prominent off the East Lothian coast, has been a fortress and a prison but is now home for countless sea birds

remnants of immense volcanic convulsions. In Glencoe, disguised as deep-slashed gullies in the towering ridges, there can still be seen the boundary marks of a volcanic accident caused when a cylinder of the upper crust collapsed into the cauldron of molten magma below. Similarly, on the road from Kilchoan to Sanna in the peninsula of Ardnamurchan in the far west, an eerie depression of peat bog and heather is circled by lava cliffs which form the finest example of a ring-dyke in Britain.

Across southern Scotland some isolated and striking rocks are the plugs of extinct volcanoes from which the softer surrounding material has long since weathered away: Dumbarton Rock, site of the hilltop capital of the ancient kingdom of Strathclyde; the Bass Rock off the East Lothian coast, once a forbidding prison for enemies of the state; and the great granite haystack of Ailsa Craig, soaring to more than 1100 ft (300 m) – 'Paddy's Milestone' to generations of Irishmen sailing up the Firth of Clyde.

Slicing diagonally across the country are two major geological fault lines. The Highland Boundary Fault, from the Firth of Clyde to near Stonehaven, is the unmistakeable division between Highland and Lowland Scotland.

The Highland Boundary Fault is even more impressive at close quarters. It is seen as a line of wooded islands crossing the southern part of Loch Lomond. Near Edzell it has formed unexpected cliffs and fissures and rock-ribs in the ravine of the River North Esk. At Comrie, which lies exactly on the fault line at the foot of Glen Lednock, the little Earthquake House has been restored, with displays showing how the science of seismography was developed in Victorian times to measure the tremors in a village which is happy to regard itself as Scotland's earthquake capital.

The other significant fault line follows the Great Glen from Fort William to Inverness, with a string of lochs in the valley it has formed between two ranges of hills – Loch Lochy, Loch Oich and the deep, enigmatic waters of Loch Ness.

There are, of course, smaller fault lines as well. The Ochil Fault, for instance, has created impressive hillsides overlooking the lower meanders of the River Forth, where pathways from villages on the landscape 'hinge' penetrate into steep-sided ravines and lead to curious formations such as a waterfall, not in the open air, but plunging down through a cavern inside the living rock.

Much later than the volcanoes and the faults there came the glaciers. Scotland's last Ice Age ended as recently as 10,000 years ago, and its traces are all around. The tangles of gravel mounds which litter many a Highland glen are moraines, the material scoured out of the rocks by the grinding motion of retreating glaciers. But the ice created landscapes on a grander scale too. The last tongue of ice, which retreated southwards down what is now Loch Lomond, excavated a deep, narrow trough at the loch's northern end. It cut across the course of a river which used to flow west to east, creating hanging valleys and a new river system.

One of the world's greatest open-air textbooks on glaciology is Glen Roy, north-east of Fort William. The so-called Parallel Roads which ring the glen – flat platforms at varying heights, each extending for miles round the horseshoe valley – baffled observers for

Flora and Fauna

When the Romans were in Scotland, and for centuries afterwards, vast areas of the country were covered by the Caledonian pine forest. Almost all of it has long since been felled or burnt down, although there are some cherished and protected remnants which have been encouraged to regenerate.

That original tree cover has gone, but 'forest' is still the word used to describe the territory of the red deer, Scotland's largest wild animal, although the deer have now adapted to grazing on bare and lonely hills. More than 150,000 of them live in Scotland, and the population is kept steady, not just in the sporting season but also by an annual cull. A sturdy red deer stag stands more than 4 ft (120 cm) tall at the withers, and usually has a forbidding display of antlers, which are grown and shed annually. The finest sets are called royals, and the occasional 14-pointers are imperials.

Red deer occur in substantial numbers in many parts of north and north-west Scotland, and on islands such as Arran, Jura and Mull. During the summer they are rarely seen in daylight near public roads, since they graze high in the corries, but late at night they may suddenly appear in a car's headlights, crossing a road on their way to drink from a river in some valley floor.

Their breeding season – the 'rut' – comes in the autumn. That is the most impressive time in deer-forest country, when the stags' roaring echoes for miles around the hills. Then the stag lives up to the title of Landseer's famous painting, *The Monarch of The Glen*.

Smaller than the red deer, the roe is essentially a creature of the woodlands. Some nature trail leaflets suggest that the areas they cover are roe deer territory, but only visitors who move quietly around near dawn or dusk are likely to glimpse one of these lovely animals, which are extremely shy during daylight hours.

There are also restricted numbers of sika deer (introduced from Japan) and of fallow deer, originally intended for parklands, which live in groups in some of the mainland counties, on Islay and Mull among the

Red deer seek grazing in the sparse winter heather

centuries. They were revealed only in mid-Victorian times as the different shore levels of a vast glacial lake, whose surface became lower as the debris which blocked the mouth of the glen gave way at intervals to let tens of millions of gallons of water escape to the sea.

These descriptions of tumultuous, landscape-forming forces should not give the impression that Scotland is all 'Caledonia stern and wild'. There are

In many areas stooks are part of the agricultural past. Here they are a foreground to the jagged ridges of the 3000 ft (900 m) Bla Bheinn, seen from the crofting village of Torrin on Skye

many acres of rich and well-worked farmlands in districts like East Lothian, Fife, Angus, Aberdeenshire, Ayrshire, the Moray Lowlands, the Solway Coast and the level Merse of Berwickshire. Moreover,

larger islands, and – a remarkable survival – on the thickly wooded island of Inchcailloch on Loch Lomond.

Feral goats are found in several parts of Scotland. Hill walkers, for instance, are sometimes surprised by them on the sides of Ben Lomond. They can also be seen in a large enclosure beside the Queens Way in the Galloway Forest Park.

Foxes and pine martens, wildcats, badgers and otters are more often noticed (and that not very often) by the traces they leave rather than by their presence. Some animals once prominent in Scotland became extinct hundreds of years ago in the wild, but wolves and bison, among others, have been brought back to the Highland Wildlife Park at Kincraig near Aviemore.

In most of Britain the grey squirrel, introduced in the 1870s from North America, has ousted the red. However, Scotland has large populations of both varieties, and red squirrels predominate in the Highland pine forests.

These attractive woodlands, which were deliberate plantations rather than natural successors to the original, are also home to a fine variety of birds. The Speyside pinewoods, for instance, have substantial numbers of woodpeckers, crossbills, chaffinches, siskins and crested tits. In an entirely different dimension there are also capercaillies, blundering into the air and making calls which sound like champagne corks popping and other sound effects from some hysterical party.

High above the pinewoods, the Cairngorm plateau is a completely different avian world. Ptarmigan survive all year round above 3000 ft (900 m), as they have done since soon after the last Ice Age, their plumage turning white to match the winter snows. Lovely little dotterels

live on the high tops in summer. The rarest bird of this sub-arctic plateau is the snow bunting, although migrants from Iceland and Scandinavia feed on lower farmlands in winter.

Iceland is also the home territory of the swans which have come every year for untold centuries to the Insh Marshes south-west of the Cairngorms. They have been reported by airline pilots as cruising at 25,000 ft (760 m)!

Scotland has several species of birds of prey. Sparrowhawks, hen harriers and buzzards are frequently found. Buzzards also perch at times on roadside telephone poles, deluding visitors into thinking they have seen a golden eagle. That much larger and most majestic of British predators is, however, a very much rarer sight, and each pair of eagles has exclusive occupation of many square miles of territory.

Among other places, Islay and the nature reserve at Caerlaverock on the Solway are world-famous wintering grounds for greylag, pinkfoot and barnacle geese. These arrive in their thousands every autumn from Spitzbergen and other Arctic breeding areas.

As well as dozens of species of loch and river birds – including, among many more familiar types, the vividly marked great northern diver found on some high-latitude lochs – Scotland has teeming populations of seabirds: gulls of every description, guillemots, kittiwakes, fulmars and the rest find nesting ledges at different levels on noisy cliff faces. On the other hand, one of the most relaxing activities imaginable is to settle by a sea-loch shore and listen to the cooing sounds from a raft of eiders.

Orkney and Shetland hold a special fascination for ornithologists, partly because they are ideally placed to

matching the rugged peaks and ridges of the rock-climbers' mountains, there are rounded grass-and-heather hill ranges like the Lammermuirs and Moorfoots, Sidlaws and Monadhliaths.

Ben Nevis, Britain's highest mountain, crouches above Fort William, but the gullies and buttresses of the approaches used by mountaineers lead to a summit plateau. The most massive of Scotland's mountain ranges, the Cairngorms, rise east of the Spey to a subarctic plateau where, among the shattered granite tors and the vast, scooped-out glacial hollows, there are no peaks, only noticeably higher points on the 4000-foot (1200-metre) high tableland.

Even the distinction between Highlands and Lowlands can be blurred. Highland Region has lowland Caithness at its northernmost tip, a county with Scotland's longest overland views, across mile upon mile of almost treeless farms and moorland to the hazy mountains on the Sutherland border.

Scotland includes more than 700 islands, and even neighbouring ones can be remarkably different from one another. In the Firth of Clyde, which also accommodates the striking granite landscapes of north Arran and Ailsa Craig, Bute is an island of gentle farms and woodlands.

Farther west, Islay has hundreds of farms, spick-and-span whitewashed villages and a scattering of whisky distilleries which make use of the pure local water and the abundant reserves of peat. Just a five-minute ferry trip away, Jura's towering, rubble-surfaced mountains and windswept moors provide thousands of acres of wildest deer-stalking country.

The archipelagos of Orkney and Shetland are quite different in appearance, the first more inclined to farming and the second to fishing. Shetland is closer to Bergen in Norway than it is to Aberdeen and – a more bizarre statistic – closer to Iceland than it is to London. It lies so far north that in the middle of the year there is no real darkness. This is the lovely time of the midnight 'simmer dim'.

One legacy that the action of winds and waves has given Scotland is its magnificent beaches. There are, of course, sands of some kind on almost every stretch of coast. But as a general rule, the best are the farthest away – Balnakeil and Invernaver, for example, on the north coast of Sutherland. On the west coasts of Lewis and Harris there are lovely, unpolluted gold or silver sands, backed by turf ablaze with wild flowers, where the green and white Atlantic breakers come creaming in.

be temporary resting grounds for birds on long-distance migrations. The National Trust for Scotland, the Royal Society for the Protection of Birds and the Nature Conservancy Council operate reserves on many individual islands.

Orkney features loch and moorland reserves, as well as the 1100-ft (335-m) cliffs of North Hoy, the screaming seabird metropolis on the Noup Cliffs of Westray, and the gentler landscape of the island of Copinsay, a reserve dedicated to the memory of the great ornithologist, James Fisher.

Arctic skuas and terns are a more common sight in Shetland than bird-watchers from southern parts of Britain are inclined to believe before their first visit, notably on the island of Unst in the far north. Fetlar, unusually green for Shetland, offers breeding colonies of plover, curlew, whimbrel and the burrowing Manx shearwaters.

In its isolated position midway between Orkney and Shetland, rugged Fair Isle is a breeding station for gannets and remarkable numbers of puffins, as well as a welcome landfall for many rare migrants. Since its takeover by the National Trust for Scotland, the island has operated its own bird observatory, attracting visitors from all over Britain and beyond.

Back on the mainland, Scotland's most recent forests are commercial plantations of spruce and larch and pine. But fine preserved oakwoods remain, in locations like Loch Lomondside, at the head of Glen Trool in Galloway, near Salen and Strontian above Loch Sunart. Birchwoods are a feature of many districts, one example on high ground being the Morrone Birkwood above Braemar, with its underlay of juniper.

The flow country of Caithness and Sutherland is under threat, as conservationists see it, from a programme of afforestation. But its flat and lonely blanket bogs and sphagnum mosses are still a habitat for rare plants like the insect-eating sundew.

Deep in dark and watery canyons like the Corrieshalloch Gorge near Ullapool, the Falls of Clyde reserve above New Lanark and Alva Glen on the south side of the Ochil Hills, ferns, sedges and lichens flourish in the damp atmosphere.

High on Ben Lawers, overlooking Loch Tay, a National Trust for Scotland reserve provides perfect conditions for ground-hugging arctic-alpine plants, where the corries sparkle in early summer with moss campion, saxifrage and mountain pansy.

At lower levels, all over the Highlands and the Southern Uplands, Scotland's most characteristic wildflower is heather, which carpets the summer and autumn hills with a warming purple glow, and is far more widespread than the official national flower, the thistle.

A quite different plant environment is the machair – the smooth and lush, abundant shell-sand turf behind the Hebridean and some northern mainland beaches. In summer the machair blooms with clover, buttercups, primroses, ragwort, chickweeds, yarrow, ladies' bedstraw and the intricate flowers of the bird's-foot trefoil. A landscape on the sometimes bleak Atlantic edge of Britain teems with colour.

A golden eagle, rare but quite unmistakeable when in flight above the crags of its territory

Countryside, Parks and Gardens

SO MUCH OF SCOTLAND is fine open country, of hill and riverside, loch and shore, moorland and forest, wildlife habitats and well-used pathways, that it has to be carefully if unobtrusively preserved. Fortunately, there are many public and private organizations, either owning, administering or simply associated in admiration of hundreds of thousands of acres of Scotland's most beautiful countryside, and whose interests include conservation and public access.

The National Trust for Scotland owns more than 100 individual properties. Some of these are modest in scope, like the Tenement House in Glasgow and cottages in the East Neuk villages of Fife. Others are on a much more majestic scale, and they include complete mountain ranges in Glencoe, Kintail and Torridon. As well as keeping the hills free for walkers and climbers, the Trust runs visitor centres which provide information about the local landscape, history and wildlife.

Adjoining the Trust's Torridon property in Wester Ross, the Nature Conservancy Council's Beinn Eighe reserve (established in 1951) was the first National Nature Reserve in Britain. It includes more individual summits, another visitor centre and two mountainside trails in an area of stunning high-level views, red and roe deer habitats, birchwoods and a remnant of the old Caledonian pine forest.

In the Central Highlands, although part of the Cairngorms range is best known for its skiing, there is a 100 square mile (260 sq km) National Nature Reserve nearby. Much of that is climbers' country, but a glorious trail through pine and larch and juniper woods circles the easily accessible Loch an Eilein.

These Speyside pine forests which rise to the foothills of the Cairngorms are among Scotland's most precious assets. Around Loch Garten, one stretch of

Culzean Castle on a cliff overlooking the Firth of Clyde is in the care of the National Trust for Scotland, while the grounds are now a country park with a network of paths in the woods behind it

Angling

Scotland has an abundance of angling rivers, lochs, reservoirs and 'fisheries'. Even if, to book a place on one of the best river locations, anglers have to make their preparations well in advance, there is almost an embarrassment of choice.

The finest rivers include the Tweed, Tay, Dee, Don, Spey, Findhorn, Oykel and Halladale. There are innumerable fishing lochs, from major areas like Loch Tay, Loch Lomond, Loch Leven and Loch Awe, to the trout lochans of the Caithness moors and the maze of tangled waterways on the map of North Uist. High latitudes are no disadvantage. The recognized angling waters in Shetland number around 1000.

There is inexpensive town-centre fishing on rivers like the Tweed in Peebles and the Tay in Perth. It was at the Glendelvine stretch of the Tay – neither inexpensive nor town-centre – where, more than 60 years ago, a young woman landed the 67½-lb (30-kg) salmon which remains the Scottish record.

The salmon is the river fish *par excellence*. Many anglers also favour the migratory sea trout, while others go for the brown trout which feeds in the same area of river or loch all its life. Scotland's rainbow trout population is almost all raised for individual fisheries, although some escape occasionally into nearby rivers, as has happened on the Annan.

Angling in Scotland almost always means game fishing. There are only a handful of coarse-fishing clubs, whose members favour pike, roach and perch.

One recognized coarse fish, however, is close to being considered a game variety. On the upper Clyde and on many of the Border rivers, grayling is a favourite winter catch, partly because its current coarse-fish status means that it has no close season like trout and salmon. Coarse fish are rarely caught for the pot, but the grayling makes a fine dish, similar to trout.

The local fishing-tackle shop, if there is one, is the place to go for advice. It will sell permits for most of the local waters, although they will be controlled by an angling association, a local authority, an estate or an anglers' hotel. In Forestry Commission areas permits are available at forest offices, caravan sites and the like.

The prices that anglers pay vary considerably. Very few rivers charging less than £10 per day provide really good returns, but it is possible to pay less than £20 for an annual trout-fishing permit on a respectable water.

An angler's fly box – and a fine salmon – beside the Tay

On the other hand the superb loch and river complexes of Garynahine and Grimersta in Lewis are owned by syndicates, and opportunities for outsiders to fish what are undoubtedly some of the finest angling waters in Europe are rare and expensive.

Estate owners and angling associations have major restocking programmes in hand. Moreover, the fact that nearly 300 of the estuary salmon-netting stations on the east coast have recently been closed is good news for all salmon anglers, who believe it to be the king of Scottish rivers rather than a bulk commercial catch.

forest owned by the Royal Society for the Protection of Birds is famous for its ospreys, the great fish-eating eagles which were hunted to extinction in this country around the turn of the century, but re-established themselves in the 1950s. Ospreys also feature in one of the Scottish Wildlife Trust's reserves at Loch of the Lowes near Dunkeld.

More of the Speyside pinewoods are included in the Forestry Commission's Glenmore Forest Park, which begins at Loch Morlich. It provides miles of walks and bridleways, has its own information centre and even offers a chance to visit Scotland's only reindeer herd.

The Commission has other major recreational facilities in the Argyll Forest Park, in the Queen Elizabeth Forest Park around the Trossachs and the eastern shore of Loch Lomond, and in its 240 square mile (640 sq km) Galloway Forest Park. These are extensive areas, with their own visitor centres, forest rangers, waymarked trails, picnic sites, fishing lochs and rivers. And many smaller forests welcome visitors too.

City parks are nothing new in Scotland. Glasgow Green dates back to medieval times, while some of Aberdeen's parkland was given to the people by Robert Bruce more than 650 years ago. More recently, the country park movement has gathered momentum. These parks are areas of woodland or moorland run by local authorities, sometimes centred on former private estates now restored under public ownership.

There are about 30 country parks in Scotland, ranging from the woods, gardens and clifftop walks around the National Trust for Scotland's castle at Culzean on the Ayrshire coast to Aden north of Aberdeen, with its handsomely restored semi-circular range of farm buildings and an exhibition which features, not just the landed family who used to own it, but also the ordinary people who worked the estate.

All the country parks make a feature of their abundant wildlife and miles of paths and nature trails, but they are also enthusiastic about their own history. Palacerigg on the moors above Cumbernauld, for

Golf

Exactly where, when and by whom the game of golf was first played is a matter of some dispute, but there is no question that in terms of facilities, equipment and the formulation of rules its development was entirely Scottish. So much golf was being played on sandy coastline turf in 15th-century Scotland that three Acts of Parliament were passed – to no noticeable effect – insisting that more time should be spent on archery practice and less on hitting a small ball with a stick into a hole.

In many countries, golf is inevitably an expensive pursuit, but this is not the case in Scotland, where there are hundreds of courses, many of them public or open to visitors. Glasgow, for example, has more than a dozen actually inside the city limits. On the other hand, some of the private clubs are among the most exclusive organizations in Scotland, and applications for membership are carefully vetted.

Courses are divided between those on coastal links and those inland, often in parkland settings. Of the coastal courses, the ones at St Andrews and Dornoch, in Ayrshire and in East Lothian, are among the finest in the world.

The town of Ayr has three courses. Troon, a little way up the coast, has five, not counting the one at Barassie just along the road. Royal Troon Golf Club's Old Course (the club runs the Portland course as well) is an Open Championship venue.

At Gullane in East Lothian, the district where a visitor is said to have remarked that ground unsuitable for golf is given over to agriculture, there are so many courses that three of them are known simply by numbers. The Luffness course directly adjoins them and Muirfield is only the length of the village away.

Television viewers in many countries watch pro-celebrity tournaments played at one of the two Turnberry Hotel courses in Ayrshire, with their spectacular views over the Firth of Clyde to Ailsa Craig and at Gleneagles, where the hotel has four courses set out in its splendid Perthshire grounds.

However, the most famous golfing location of all is St Andrews, which has five courses and is contemplating the building of a sixth. To play on the Old Course at St Andrews is every golfer's dream, and any player with a reasonable handicap can in fact do so. The course is owned by a public trust, and its green fees appear incredibly cheap to foreign visitors.

There is nothing fancy here: no lines of specially planted trees (in fact, there are no trees at all), no flamboyant shrubbery, no artificially created lakes, no landscape gardening and no carefully flattened fairways.

As a promotional exercise for golf, the Old Course has, apart from the finest and best-kept natural turf in the world, little to recommend it. There are fairways with wicked dips, humps and depressions, massive, magnificently tended greens and awkwardly placed sand-filled bunkers with all-too appropriate names such as Hell, Coffin and Grave. Also in its favour is the fact

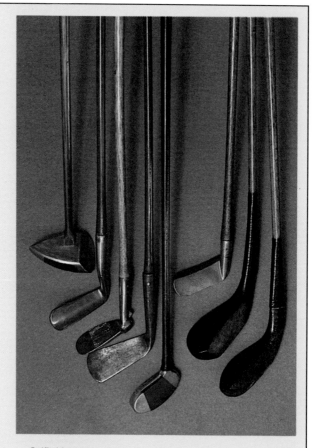

Golf's history is recalled in a dedicated museum at St Andrews

that the finest players in the world have been tested here – by the links themselves and by the unpredictable wind. Most top-ranking professionals consider the 17th hole at St Andrews to be the most difficult in the game.

Overlooking the first tee and the 18th green are the baronial-style headquarters of the Royal and Ancient Golf Club – not the oldest club, but by far the most influential. It was a suggestion by the Royal and Ancient in 1764 when it put forward a plan to rearrange the previous layout which led to the standardization of the golf course length at 18 holes. Although it now shares the framing of the Rules of Golf with the very much younger United States Golf Association, it has made a move to extend its influence much farther afield.

One American astronaut took a club and ball to the Moon, and was seen on television in his bulky space-suit playing the first-ever golf shot on the sandy lunar surface. The Royal and Ancient sent him a message of congratulations, but noted that he would be penalized one stroke, having been observed – from a quarter of a million miles away – contravening the rule about grounding his club in a bunker.

example, has displays illustrating its former existence as a labour colony, until the 1930s a place of work for otherwise unemployed men who were brought daily by train from Glasgow. Lochore Meadows Country Park in Fife, created with massive local effort in the 1970s, recalls its previous surroundings as a wasteland of coal-mining debris.

Between Dunbar and Tyninghame in East Lothian, the John Muir Country Park extends along 8 miles (13 km) of coastline, and is a reminder, in its name, of the local man who was one of the pioneers of the national park movement in the United States.

Many private estates play their part in keeping the countryside open. Bowhill near Selkirk has nature trails alongside the beautiful Yarrow Water. Monteviot north of Jedburgh provides a multitude of waymarked walks, one reaching a marvellous Border view-point, the soaring Waterloo Monument on the summit of Peniel Heugh. At Glentanar on Deeside the estate's visitor centre, situated beside a river flanked

Scottish cooking

With some of the world's finest Aberdeen-Angus beef herds, fresh trout and salmon from the rivers, grouse from the moors, wide acres of vegetable farms and a ring of white-fish ports, Scotland's cooks – even if they do not always take advantage of them – have high-quality ingredients ready to hand.

At its best, traditional household cooking in Scotland is plainer than many continental styles, and certainly not intended for the mere nibbler. Soup, especially in the form of vegetable-packed Scotch broth, is of a consistency in which spoons almost stand upright. Particularly in winter, it is intended to 'stick to the ribs' – like oatmeal porridge – and certainly provides a warming glow.

Beef and lamb are the principal local meats, although venison, once almost entirely exported to countries such as West Germany, is available from some of the recently established commercial red deer farms.

Most of the stories told about haggis – including the one about there being a close season for shooting them, or the claim that they have legs shorter on one side than on the other to help them run round hillsides without falling over – are strictly for the tourists. But this protein-packed sheep-based dish, whose precise contents are perhaps not to be detailed for the squeamish, has been called the first well-packaged convenience food.

Fish features prominently in the Scottish kitchen. Salmon, either fresh or smoked, can be at least as good in Scotland as it is anywhere in the world.

Kippers – smoked herring – are a long-time favourite. The east-coast port of Arbroath is famous for its smokies, which are haddock deliciously cured over a beechwood fire.

Shellfish of many kinds are a significant Scottish export. Consignments are flown to the best restaurants in London and Paris. But there are West Highland hotels which must have the freshest fish and shellfish

Traditional Scots fare. In the foreground is a rich Scotch Bun or Black Bun (baked for Hogmanay), while ranged behind it are pancakes, Partan Bree soup ('partan' is crab), Scotch bun, oatcakes, beef collops and Atholl Brose, an oatmeal, whisky and honey mixture

possible, landed at harbours just a five-minute walk from the kitchen door.

The best Ayrshire potatoes melt in the mouth. And the extensive soft-fruit production around Blairgowrie has made that town the 'raspberry capital' of Europe.

Traditional Scottish recipes persist. There is a fine crab soup called partan bree. Cock-a-leekie is soup made from chicken, bacon, herbs, leeks and prunes. Cullen skink is another fish affair with finnan haddock, milk, potato and onion. Now spreading to the mainland, clapshot is an old Orkney recipe in which the simple-sounding combination of mashed potato and Swedish turnip, well mixed with roast dripping and perhaps a pinch or two of chives, is regarded by enthusiasts as a splendid side dish.

Scotland has developed famous cheeses in the past, like Dunlop and Orkney. Crowdie is a soft cottage cheese and Caboc a cream cheese rolled in oatmeal.

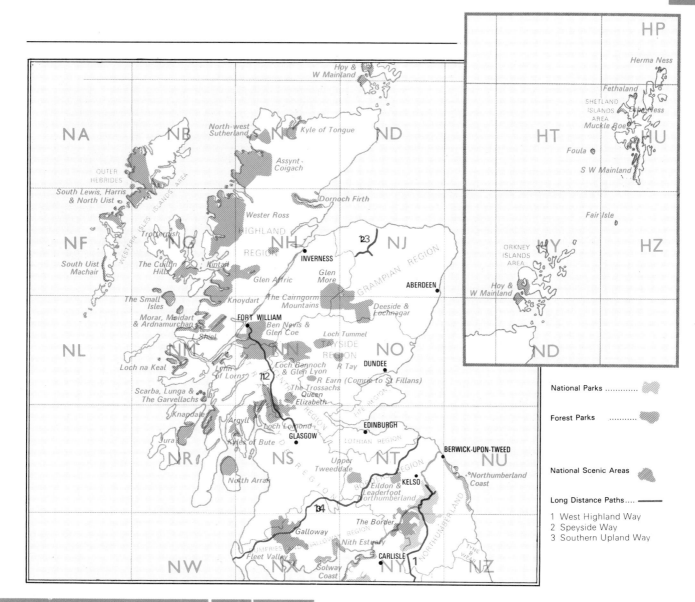

National Parks ....

Forest Parks ....

National Scenic Areas

Long Distance Paths.... ———

1 West Highland Way
2 Speyside Way
3 Southern Upland Way

The harbour of the charming little Fife royal burgh of Pittenweem

by lovely wooded hills, is on the site of a village which made its living by offering food, drink, accommodation and shoe repairs to travellers on a once-busy track crossing the Grampians.

North-west of Aberdeen, the striking hill range of Bennachie is famous for its heathery tracks following ancient pathways, its wildlife, its history of property disputes and its spectacular main summit of shattered granite blocks. A few years ago Forestry Commission officials, private landowners and keen hill walkers formed an organization, called the Bailies of Bennachie, to conserve and protect the hills, maintain the footpaths and avoid clashes of interest among the different groups whose work and recreation take them there.

The Scottish law of trespass is more liberal than is the case in England and Wales. That being said, while moorland and mountain paths may be walked taking care to avoid damage to property and the natural

Whisky

Whisky is commercially very important in Scotland, not least because foreign companies which have tried to create the precise flavour and bouquet of 'Scotch' in an alien environment have usually failed. Although whisky is often thought of as a predominantly Highland product, there are distilleries both north and south of the Highland Line, as well as on several islands. Indeed, the biggest distillery of them all, Johnnie Walker's, was founded in the Lowland town of Kilmarnock in 1820.

The really big producers market carefully balanced blended whiskies. Blended whisky is a blend of a number of malt whiskies with grain whiskies: malt whisky is made with malted barley while grain whisky is made not just with barley, malted or otherwise, but also maize. It is in the single-malt distilleries that the mystique of whisky comes to the fore. These malt whiskies are unblended, and enthusiasts recognize in them almost as many subtleties as do connoisseurs of the wines of France.

Every malt whisky is called after the place where the distillery is located, which explains the roll-call of impressive names like Glenlivet, Glenfarclas, Glenfiddich, Macallan, Strathisla, Laphroaig and Tamdhu. Each distillery has its own special, pure and carefully tended water supply from springs or mountain burns, a major element in the distinctive taste which cannot be duplicated exactly elsewhere. Although many of these distilleries now buy malted barley from commercial maltings, others continue the old process of turning their barley on their own malting floor, heated by a peat fire below.

Traditional copper pot stills at the Glenfiddich Distillery, Dufftown

Most distilleries retain the 'pagoda' roofs which include the ventilation towers of the malt-drying kilns. These and the gleaming copper stills are the characteristic features of a traditional malt distillery, together with the oak casks – if possible, previously used for sherry – in which the young spirit is matured for years. Although the basic processes may be the same, each distillery has its own individual appeal and its own sense of history.

Distilleries in many areas provide visitor centres and guided tours, from Edradour near Pitlochry – the smallest in the whole of Scotland – to the Whisky Trail which includes in its itinerary several of the best-known Speyside names.

environment, landowners can and do impose restrictions on access, for example during the grouse-shooting season, for deer-stalking and farming and forestry work. They also have a legal remedy against any person causing damage on or to their land and may use reasonable force to remove such a person. The following simple guidelines should therefore be followed: obey restricted access notices and if asked to leave, do so; always take care to avoid damaging property and the natural environment; if you are not clear about the right of access seek permission of the landowner first.

For over a century the Scottish Rights of Way Society has maintained careful records of recognized footpaths and taken action to safeguard well-established routes against threats of closure. In the last twenty years Local Authorities have also played an active part in signposting public footpaths.

In the 1970s attention was given to creating a series of properly signposted long-distance footpaths. The first of these footpaths was the West Highland Way, which runs for 95 miles (150 km) from Milngavie north of Glasgow to Fort William, via the track bed of the old Blane Valley railway, the Loch Lomondside oakwoods and Glen Falloch. It then follows a long-abandoned military road of the 1750s which crosses the edge of Rannoch Moor, climbs the hairpin bends of Devil's Staircase out of Glencoe, dips down to Kinlochleven and then makes a final climb and descent through Glen Nevis. The Southern Upland Way, which is even longer, begins as a flight of steps for holidaymakers up

the North Cliff at Portpatrick near Stranraer and eventually finishes 212 miles (340 km) away at Cockburnspath back from the Berwickshire coast. The third of the special footpaths is the Speyside Way, which starts at a restored fishermen's icehouse on the pebbly shore of Spey Bay and follows the beautiful river valley miles inland.

Motorists, walkers, climbers, bird-watchers, picnickers, historians, sportsmen, antiquarians, children at play and people simply wanting fresh air and beautiful views will discover that the Scottish countryside has room for them all.

A winter view across Loch Torridon to the 3456 ft (1054 m) Liathach and 3232 ft (985 m) Beinn Alligin

Placenames

DISTANT GENERATIONS OF NORSEMEN, Picts and Scots from Ireland have left their marks on the rich and often confusing tapestry of Scottish placenames. So have the people of the old Saxon kingdom of Northumbria which, until the major move southwards of the Scottish border to the Tweed in 1018, extended as far north as Edinburgh and the Firth of Forth. The church of Abercurnig, for example, mentioned by St Bede, is still at Abercorn near South Queensferry.

Gaelic names, some of which have themselves been Anglicized, are mostly descriptive of the landscape. Prefixes are a good guide. 'Ard' as in Ardnamurchan means 'high ground', often a promontory. 'Inver' indicates the mouth of a river: Inverness is at the mouth of the River Ness.

'Ach' or 'Auch' is a field. Achnashellach on the Kyle of Lochalsh railway is the 'Field of Willows', and the property called Auch on the road to Glen Coe has always been farmland.

References to hills feature prominently. 'Ben' and 'Beinn' both mean 'mountain'. 'Brae' is general upland country – Braemar means the heights of the province of Mar. *Druim* is Gaelic for a ridge, which is why the name of the village of Drymen really refers to its position rather than to the 'three dry men' used to advertise one of its hotels.

In an associated allusion, the word 'Spittal', which appears in several placenames, describes a refuge or hospice for travellers, often in lonely – and inhospitable – country. Spittal of Glenshee offered shelter to travellers on the Cairnwell Pass, while Dalnaspidal on the Drumochter Pass was the 'Meadow of the Hospice', just as Dalry was originally *Dal Righ*, the 'Field' or 'Meadow of the King'.

In Orkney and Shetland, Caithness, Sutherland and the Western Isles, Norse names are frequently found. Islands like Bernera and Eriskay have the Norse suffix ('-a', '-ay' or '-ey') for islands in their names. Many of these words include a personal name, but Jura was then, as it still is today, Deer Island. The name Oronsay is used for an island linked at low tide to some larger land mass.

Skerry, a rugged sea rock or stretch of rocks covered by the sea at high water is derived from the Norse 'sker'. Muckle Skerry in Shetland and Scarfskerry on the north coast of Caithness are examples. 'Stakkr', the Norse for hill or precipitous rock appears as 'Stack' or 'Staca', for example Stackaberg and Stack of Sumra in Shetland and Stacashel in the Western Isles. Many place names in one-time Viking country end in '-ster': Lybster, Occumster and Scrabster. This suffix is derived from the Norse *bolstathr*, a homestead.

Occasionally, Norse and Gaelic come together in a hybrid name. Mellon Udrigle sounds bizarre, but this beautifully situated Wester Ross village, looking over sand-dunes and a sea-loch towards the mountains of Coigach (any name with 'Coig' refers to an old land-division into fifths) contains a Norse personal name and a Gaelic landscape description as 'Idrigill's Little Hill.'

Scottish placenames, like many others, have their snares and delusions. Gleneagles has nothing to do with birds of prey. 'Eagles' in this instance is from the Gaelic *eaglais*, meaning 'a church'.

Norse- or Gaelic-speaking sailors who knew its angry waters well might appreciate the modern name of Cape Wrath, but in Gaelic the district around it is still called the Parph, from the original Norse *hvarf*, a turning-point on voyages to and from the Northern and the Western Isles.

Accurate pronunciation of Gaelic names is a difficult thing for non-Gaelic speakers to achieve and impossible to describe in a short essay. As just one example, there is a mountain above Glen Creran in Argyll whose name is pronounced 'Benoola'. It is written as Beinn Fhionnlaidh.

Borders

VISITORS TO KELSO may be puzzled by the fact that, marked on the surface of its elegant Georgian square, there is the location of an old Bull Ring. Toreadors never flourished here, but **Kelso** was and is one of the great livestock-market towns of Scotland. It also provides for many sporting activities, from the rugby matches which are a major interest in the Borders to horse-racing and angling – Kelso is where the Teviot joins the Tweed at the famous Junction Pool.

On the outskirts, Floors Castle is open regularly to visitors. This seat of the Duke of Roxburghe has lavish furnishings and art collections in its public rooms, and events ranging from massed pipe band displays to carriage driving are held in its parkland grounds.

Kelso's ruined 12th-century abbey is an ancient monument. The nearby Turret House documents the abbey's history and has other displays including a reconstructed skinner's workshop.

The route crosses the Tweed bridge, winds uphill and turns abruptly right at **Maxwellheugh** to leave Kelso on the A698, then follows the A68 into the narrow valley of the Jed Water and the handsomely restored town centre of **Jedburgh**. There is another notable ruined abbey here, as well as a mock but realistic castle built in the 1820s as a jail and now a museum of the enlightened (in terms of what had gone before) penal standards it applied. Queen Mary's House, occupied for a few days in 1566 by Mary Queen

of Scots who was in the town attending a circuit court, is now a museum devoted to her.

Leaving Jedburgh by the climbing Castlegate, the route follows the B6358 over the hills to rejoin the A698 as it approaches **Denholm**. An ornate memorial to the locally born John Leyden – poet and orientalist, and friend of Sir Walter Scott – stands on the handsomely proportioned village green.

Immediately south of Denholm, the steeply rising Rubers Law was one of the hills on which 17th-century Covenanters worshipped in secret; dawn services in memory of them are held on the summit every year. Denholm's days as a centre of the stocking-weaving trade have long since gone, although one of the old stocking mills survives, converted into a private house.

Textiles, however, are still big business in **Hawick**, the administrative centre of Roxburgh District and noted for its enthusiasm for rugby. A mansion house museum in riverside Wilton Park has displays on the development of the industry.

Heading north on the A7, the route goes over an attractive stretch of undulating hill and dale to **Selkirk**, another textile-and-rugby town on a hillside above the Yarrow Water. In its square there is a statue of Sir Walter Scott, outside the courthouse where he often

Smailholm Tower, in a setting which belies much of the gentle Borders scenery, has strong Scott associations

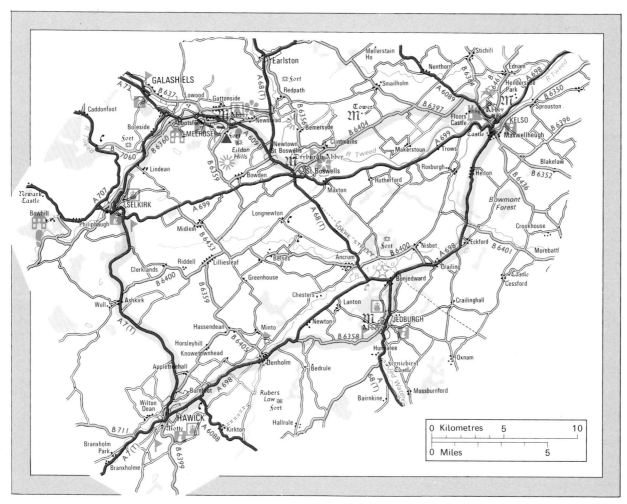

0 Kilometres 5 10

0 Miles 5

sat in judgement, and where mementos of his days on the bench are preserved. Halliwell's House Museum, in an alleyway off the square, is a re-created old-style ironmonger's shop. The first-floor galleries feature local history displays.

West of Selkirk, off the main route, **Bowhill** is the Borders home of the Duke of Buccleuch. The mansion house itself, which contains internationally acclaimed displays of paintings, porcelain and furniture, is open for six weeks every summer. Its pleasant woodland grounds, with two nature trails, open earlier in the year.

Leaving Selkirk to the north, on the A7, the route turns right on to the B6360, following the heavily wooded banks of the Tweed to **Abbotsford**, the home, built to his own detailed specifications, of Sir Walter Scott in his role as a warm-hearted Border laird. Most of the public rooms are exactly as he knew them.

Turning on to the A6091, the route reaches **Melrose**, one of the most beautifully located of the Border towns, with the triple-peaked Eildon Hills soaring up to the south. Melrose has another impressive ruined abbey. Beside it, the National Trust for Scotland's Priorwood Garden specializes in flowers for drying and in the propagation of historic strains of apple trees which the monks and, even earlier the Romans, grew.

Melrose rugby ground at the Greenyards has a famous sevens tournament every year. It was here, in fact, that the shorter version of the game was invented. There are mellow walks beside the Tweed and a motor museum in one of the streets leading to the river.

The A6091 turns right on to the A68 at **Newtown St Boswells**, and then, at **St Boswells** itself, there is a left turn on to the B6404. St Boswells has an extensive village green, attractive houses and the finest concentration of public footpaths for miles around. One of them leads to a footbridge across the Tweed towards the most beautifully situated of all the ruined Border abbeys. Dryburgh Abbey is the burial-place – by family right – of Sir Walter Scott.

East of St Boswells the route crosses a bridge over the Tweed, where steps lead down to riverside footpaths. Shortly after that, on the right, are the wooded grounds of the 18th-century Mertoun House.

The house itself is not open to visitors, but on summer weekends the gardens are, with their lovely walks, herbaceous borders, lawns, flowering shrubs, an arboretum and a circular dovecot dated to 1567. Mertoun parish church nestles in the woodlands.

Farther along the B6404, on the hillside to the left, Smailholm Tower occupies an unexpectedly craggy location. This ancient monument offers an extensive view, and has displays of costumed figures and tapestries illustrating Sir Walter Scott's *Minstrelsy of the Scottish Borders*.

Scott knew Smailholm well as a child, because his grandfather farmed nearby, and this was where he absorbed the old Border tales worked into so many of his ballads and novels. As the route returns to Kelso, it is not unreasonable that the last personality to figure in it should be the most famous Borderer of them all.

Galloway

KIRKCUDBRIGHT WAS ORIGINALLY NAMED after the church dedicated to St Cuthbert, an allusion which neither its spelling nor its pronunciation (*Kirr-coobry*, with the accent on the second syllable) makes clear. The Stewartry Museum has acquired a remarkable variety of collections on the history, wildlife, artists' and craftsmen's work, transport, shipping, militaria and almost every other imaginable subject connected with the town.

Many wealthy landed families built themselves town mansions here, the most extravagant being the 16th-century McLellan's Castle. Now partly ruined, it is preserved as an ancient monument. Later, some elegant Georgian houses were built. Notable among them is Broughton House, owned more recently by the Australian-born artist Edward Hornel. On his death in 1933 he bequeathed the house, and many of his paintings and books, to the town; it is now a museum.

Over the years, many artists have come to live and work in Kirkcudbright, and some fictional ones figured in Dorothy L. Sayers's thriller *Five Red Herrings*. Members of the present-day artists' colony exhibit in the Harbour Gallery beside the River Dee.

Leaving Kirkcudbright on the A755, the route makes for **Gatehouse of Fleet**, a town recently by-passed by the A75. It has fine Georgian buildings, notably in Ann Street, and some which are now private houses but served more utilitarian purposes in the decades after 1790 when Gatehouse was a flourishing cotton town.

On the south-eastern edge of Gatehouse, some of

Threave Castle, built in the 14th Century, was the last of the Douglas strongholds to surrender to James II, and it also fell to a Covenanter siege in 1640. It stands on an island in the Dee which is also a wildfowl refuge

the finest broadleaved-woodland walks in Galloway surround the nursery area of the Fleet Forest. To the south-west, as the town road meets the bypass, the ancient monument of the 15th-century Cardoness Castle stands on an ash-tree hill overlooking the mouth of the Fleet.

A little way farther on, beside a loop of old main road which has now been bypassed, Skyreburn Aquarium has display tanks of river, loch and sea fish found in Galloway waters. As it passes the narrow side road on the right which climbs to the Neolithic chambered cairns of Cairn Holy, and then on the left passes another ancient monument at the 16th-century tower house of Carsluith Castle, the A75 provides wide-ranging views over Wigtown Bay.

The recently bypassed **Creetown** is the location of several craft and jewellery workshops, and also of the outstanding Gem Rock Museum, housed in a redundant school. At **Palnure** a side road on the right leads to the waymarked trails in Kirroughtree Forest.

After a bridge across the River Cree, the route turns into the shopping and market town of **Newton Stewart**. Like Kirkcudbright, it has a good, voluntary-run local museum. There are riverside walks and gardens not noticed by the casual passer-by.

Leaving Newton Stewart along the A714, the route follows the west bank of the Cree until turning right on to a minor road, crossing the river and coming to a junction on the far side. The road straight ahead here leads to Glen Trool, with its miles of forest walks and magnificent viewpoints over Loch Trool. The main route, however, turns right after crossing the Cree, to follow a winding riverside road into the RSPB's Wood of Cree nature reserve, where footpaths from a grassy car park explore one of the finest oakwoods in Galloway.

Back in a built-up area, the fine old village of **Minnigaff** is now a suburb of Newton Stewart, although it was once a burgh in its own right. Beyond Minnigaff the A712 is a road with many abrupt corners as it goes through one of the major plantation areas of the Galloway Forest Park.

The area becomes more open at the start of the Queens Way. A steep forest trail climbs to the long-abandoned Edinburgh-Wigtown coach road, in an area of waterfalls and old lead mines. Farther along the Queens Way there are a wild goat park and a red deer enclosure.

The Raiders Road forest drive (summer only) is off to the right immediately after the bridge over the Black Water of Dee, and on the left, beside Clatteringshaws Loch, the Galloway Deer Museum has displays on local forestry, on the generation of hydroelectricity and on more kinds of wildlife than its name suggests.

New Galloway used to be Scotland's smallest royal burgh, until that status was abolished in the local government reorganization of 1975. Here the route crosses the Water of Ken and turns right on to the A713, running alongside the long and narrow Loch

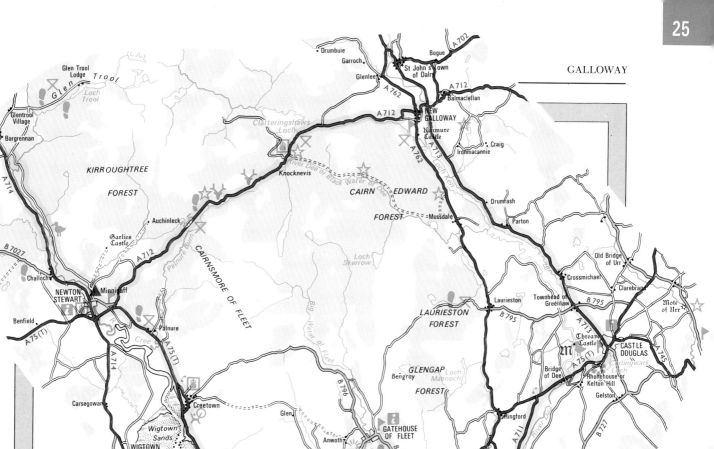

The gardens at Threave are part of an estate in the care of the National Trust for Scotland. Several representative gardens have been developed within the grounds, by students at the School of Practical Gardening, and these are open to visitors

Ken, a fine place for bird-watching. Off to the left, Blowplain Farm offers friendly guided tours.

At **Castle Douglas** the route comes to a major market town. Turning right on to the busy A75, it leads very shortly to the more tranquil edge of the town, where villas overlook a pleasant public park at Carlingwark Loch.

On both sides of the A75 south-west of Castle Douglas, places called Threave attract the attention. To the left, the National Trust for Scotland's Threave Gardens are where many of its own gardeners are trained. To the right there are observation points on the Threave Wildfowl Refuge, a favourite wintering ground for geese and ducks, and a ferry-crossing to one of Galloway's most imposing ancient monuments – the 14th-century Threave Castle, the island fortress of the Douglases on the River Dee.

Turning on to the A711, the route follows the west bank of the Dee, back towards Kirkcudbright. At **Tongland** there are guided tours of the last of the chain of hydroelectric power stations strung all the way down river from the Ayrshire border.

In a district where angling is not the least important of life's activities, the power station complex includes a carefully built, multi-level salmon ladder so that the fish are not cut off from their spawning grounds far up in the hills.

Edinburgh

ALTHOUGH IT HAS NOT BEEN a seat of government since the Treaty of Union in 1707, Edinburgh is still unmistakeably a capital city. Official departments operating with comparative freedom of action, legal and financial firms, publishers, politicians, city clubs, company headquarters, important galleries and museums – all these help to enhance Edinburgh's status.

Every August it plays host to theatre, music, dance and art from all over the world in the Edinburgh International Festival which, some years ago, was so packed with major events that a Festival Fringe was created to accommodate smaller groups.

In its setting and in much of its central architecture, the city has few rivals in Europe. High above the shops and gardens of Princes Street, Edinburgh Castle stands outlined on the summit of its volcanic crag. From the castle, down the Royal Mile to the Palace of Holyroodhouse, the Old Town of Edinburgh is full of historic buildings, museums, shops and intriguing alleyways.

When the Old Town became far too cramped for the increasing population, Edinburgh's 18th-century city fathers commissioned the creation of two Georgian 'New Towns', which survive in remarkably unsullied form as one of the great townscapes of the world.

As a significant settlement, Edinburgh predates by far any of its surviving buildings, and is considerably older than Scotland itself. Early in the 7th century King Edwin of Northumbria had a fortress on what is now the Castle Rock, but that and the defensive works of much earlier, nameless tribes have long since been buried under the imposing masonry seen today.

At the heart of the present-day castle is the tiny St Margaret's Chapel, accommodating not many more than 20 people at services which have been held there for more than 900 years. That is the oldest part of the castle, which has spread out over the whole area at the top of the rock, and is one of Scotland's major attractions for visitors. During the Festival the world-famous Military Tattoo is held on the castle esplanade.

The most characteristic part of the Old Town is the Royal Mile, which is not an address at all and does not appear on many maps of the city. It is made up of the Castlehill, the Lawnmarket, High Street and Canongate, each lower than the preceding one, until the Royal Mile finally comes to an end at Holyroodhouse.

One of the best detailed views of Edinburgh is from the Camera Obscura in the Outlook Tower on Castlehill. A short stroll away, there are four quite different museums in the Royal Mile. Lady Stair's House is a 17th-century building devoted to three of Scotland's most prominent literary figures – Robert Burns, Sir

One of the most famous of all urban views – Edinburgh Castle, Waverley Station, the National Gallery of Scotland, the Scott Monument and Princes Street with its fashionable shops

Walter Scott and Robert Louis Stevenson. The Museum of Childhood in the High Street was the first one in the world with this particular theme. Huntly House in the Canongate is where Edinburgh displays material about its own history, its industries, its old shop signs, and the silver and glassware for which it has been known for years.

Unlike the others, the Canongate Tolbooth is more concerned with temporary exhibitions, but it has a fine collection of tartans, and also offers the opportunity to make stone and brass rubbings from exact replicas of famous originals.

Open to visitors for most of the year, the Palace of Holyroodhouse is the Queen's official residence in Scotland. It stands on the edge of Holyrood Park, which sweeps up by lava cliffs and steep grassy slopes to the summit of Arthur's Seat, from which there is a glorious view over the city and its surroundings.

Edinburgh is fortunate in its parks, which also include hillsides round the observatory at Blackford, the little river valley at the Hermitage of Braid, and the wooded ridge with pleasant high-level pathways on Corstorphine Hill.

One of the finest walks follows the Water of Leith, the river which winds unobtrusively through Edinburgh from the south-west and once powered more than 70 mills employed in the production of paper, timber, flour and snuff.

Right in the heart of the city, the river flows past Dean Village, a lovely complex of 17th- and 18th-century buildings where once the baxters – or bakers – of Edinburgh went about their business.

Edinburgh, in fact, only masquerades as a city. It is really a central town with a ring of villages on its periphery, even if the villages, administratively speaking, are now its suburbs. Duddingston still has memories of the time when Bonnie Prince Charlie lodged there. Generations before then one of his Stuart ancestors who did manage to occupy the throne used to relax with a game of skittles in the Sheep Heid Inn. People still play skittles today in a pub whose history goes back 600 years.

Currie, Colinton and Juniper Green are all clearly defined villages along the Water of Leith. The city's north-western boundary is at Cramond, the beautifully restored, former oyster-fishermen's village at the mouth of the River Almond, where Celts and Romans, Baltic traders, bishops and monarchs have come and gone in the last 2000 years, all leaving traces behind.

Much of the time, however, the visitor's eye tends to be drawn to the hills which rise to the south. The hamlet of Swanston, where Robert Louis Stevenson spent much of his boyhood, is part of Edinburgh, but lies out of the general built-up area in the foothills of the Pentlands.

Edinburgh's part of the Pentland range rises to the summits of Caerketton and Allermuir, which Stevenson remembered with affection in distant Samoa. From the public park at Bonaly, family parties often walk towards the spectacular scenery, reminiscent of the Highlands, at the reservoirs of Torduff and Clubbiedean.

As well as all its city-centre attractions, Edinburgh also offers breezy pathways on grass and heather hills.

Edinburgh Castle, on the ridge of the old town, has commanding views over the city. The bridge across the dry moat leads to the outer gate, flanked by figures of Bruce and Wallace

Lammermuir Hills

LEAVING EDINBURGH ON THE A1, this tour turns south for **Dalkeith** and, at Church Street on the edge of the town, reaches a parking area for the two attractive nature trails in the well-wooded grounds of Dalkeith Park estate. Footpaths, driveways and forest tracks follow the banks of the North and South Esk rivers.

Beyond Dalkeith the A68 crosses a five-arched Telford bridge into the hillside village of **Pathhead** and then climbs steadily, eventually giving long views down over the rich farmlands in the East Lothian plain and across the Firth of Forth.

Off to the right, as the main road takes the steeper gradient to the tableland beyond Soutra Hill, the B6368 leads shortly to Soutra Aisle, all that remains of a 12th-century hospice for travellers and pilgrims. Even now these uplands can be harsh places in wild winter weather.

After sweeping down the far side of **Soutra**, bordered on the left by the steep grassy banks of the Lammermuir foothills, the route turns on to the A697, bypassing the town of **Lauder**. To the right, in the valley of the Leader Water, the red-sandstone Thirlestane Castle is a flamboyant Restoration design with superb plaster ceilings, valuable paintings and ceramics. Part of the castle complex has been turned into the extensive Border Country Life Museum.

At the end of a straight but undulating stretch of moorland farms and roadside plantations, the A697 reaches **Greenlaw**, which has some unexpectedly ambitious buildings for a place with no major status. The explanation for this is that for many years, until the struggle was lost in 1903, it vied with Duns for the honour of being the county town of Berwickshire. Even what looks like the church tower is not the church tower at all, but an attached building which once served as the county jail.

After Greenlaw, on the tree-lined A6105 for Duns, there is a worthwhile turn-off on the right leading to the historic and isolated Polwarth Kirk, standing in estate farmland above a little burn.

Duns itself is a fine, solid Border county town. In Newtown Street the Jim Clark Memorial Room displays many of the trophies awarded to the Berwickshire farmer who twice won the title of World Champion racing driver. Duns Castle grounds are now a nature reserve, and from the Castle Street entrance a footpath climbs to the summit of Duns Law, from which there is a widespread view over the patchwork of farms in the Merse of Berwickshire, with the Cheviot Hills rising to the English border.

Thirlestane Castle outside Lauder shows the architectural styles of the 16th, 17th and 19th Centuries, the 1590 castle forming the core

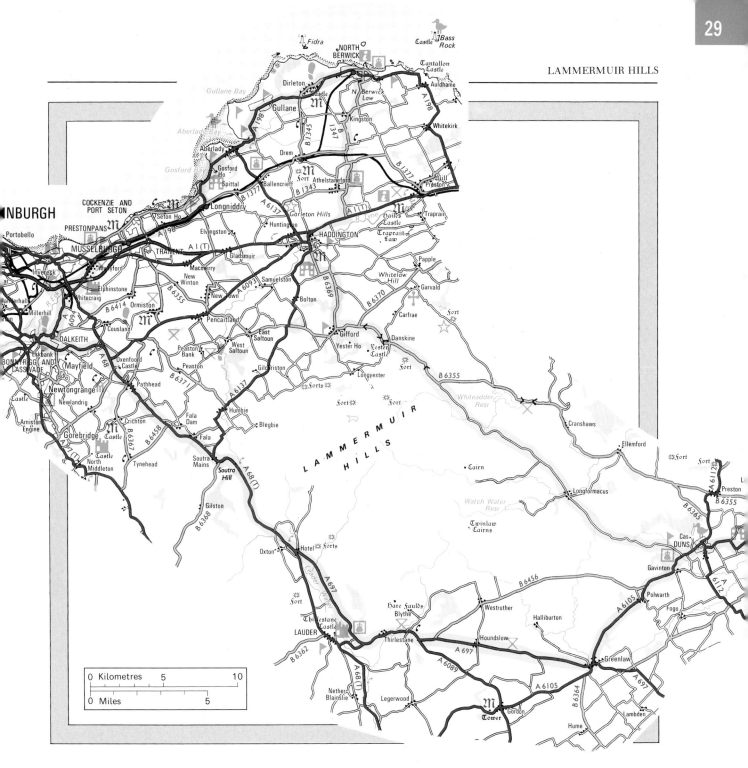

A mile or so east of Duns, off the A6105 as it continues towards Berwick-upon-Tweed, lies Manderston, one of the most amazing mansions in Britain, built at the turn of the century. Its millionaire owner told his architect what every architect wants to hear: money is no object. So the interior is lavishly furnished, and the stables were probably designed as the most extravagant racehorse accommodation in the world. House and gardens are open at regular but limited times during the summer.

The route retraces its steps from Duns, back south-west along the A6105, before turning up past Duns golf course to begin the climb on a minor road by the lonely village of **Longformacus** into the heart of the Lammermuirs. This is a landscape of rounded grass and heather-covered hills, moorland burns and distant sheep farms.

Going straight on onto the B6355, the route dips down into the pleasantly arranged 18th-century village of **Gifford**. It has houses on both sides of a wide avenue of lime trees, an old market cross in the tiny square and a whitewashed parish church with some notable memorials.

North of Gifford there is mature estate country around Lennoxlove House, the seat of the Duke of Hamilton. The house is open to visitors on certain days. Guided tours reveal mementos of Mary Queen of Scots, whose private secretary owned it in the days when it was called Lethington. The present name was decided upon by a later owner, 'La Belle Stuart' – the Duchess of Richmond and Lennox, one-time mistress of Charles II.

The county town of **Haddington** is the focus of a remarkable conservation effort, most of its Georgian buildings having been sensitively restored. It is best explored on foot by way of its fascinating town trail.

Turning briefly on to the A1, the route soon leaves it again for the B1347. Off to the left is the conservation village of **Athelstaneford**, near where a 10th-century Scottish/Pictish army, according to a long-standing tradition, saw in the sky a white St Andrew's cross against a blue background. That became and remains the national flag of Scotland, celebrated in a display at the parish church.

The Museum of Flight at East Fortune is on the right. It was an airship base during World War I, and the place from which the Scottish-built R34 set off in 1919 on its pioneer double crossing of the Atlantic. Open in summer, the museum features aircraft as diverse in scale and performance as a Puss Moth, a 1934 Weir autogiro, a Spitfire and a Vulcan bomber.

Passing immediately west of North Berwick Law, whose summit offers a dramatic view to the Bass Rock after a stiffish climb, the route enters the holiday, golf and sailing resort of **North Berwick**. Shellfish boats still use the harbour, and the town's long fishing heritage is illustrated in the local museum.

Just off the A198, Dirleton's fine 13th-century castle is open as an ancient monument. Trim cottages and the parish church face the village green. Towards the coast, an intriguing nature trail at Yellowcraig gives close-up views of the little lighthouse island of Fidra.

West of Dirleton, **Gullane** is surrounded by golf courses. On the seaward side, there are invigorating walks around sand-dunes still in the process of being

Haddington is a quiet country town, notable for its carefully preserved Georgian buildings and streets while among older buildings, St Mary's Parish church where John Knox worshipped has been restored. The nunnery which gave this 17th Century Nungate Bridge across the Tyne its name no longer exists

stabilized after years of neglect.

At the junction after the last of the Gullane golf courses a side road leads to the motor museum at Myreton. Continuing along the A198, the route runs alongside the nature reserve at Aberlady Bay.

Aberlady itself is a charming village with many well-maintained 18th-century houses and another historic parish church. Beyond it, northerly winds have shaped the boundary woodlands of Gosford estate. Gosford House, home of the Earl of Wemyss, has an imposing 19th-century marble hall and is occasionally open to visitors.

Zigzagging inland at **Longniddry**, the route passes a striking but not often visited ancient monument, the substantial 14th-century Seton Collegiate Church.

Off towards the coast is one of the finest industrial heritage sites in the country. The Scottish Mining Museum at Prestongrange shows records of coalmining there going back almost 800 years. It has an exhibition hall, a majestic old beam engine and industrial locomotives which are regularly run 'in steam'.

Not far away, the route rejoins the A1 at the Musselburgh bypass and returns to Edinburgh.

Glasgow

GLASGOW is now in the midst of an exciting programme of restoration and transformation. This process would have attracted the approval of the wealthy 19th-century industrialists who made Glasgow the second city of the Empire, but it began in fact in a much lower key, when repairs had to be made to many buildings in the wake of the hurricane of January 1968.

The holding of the National Garden Festival here in 1988, and Glasgow's status as the European City of Culture in 1990, are merely two of the major elements in far-seeing plans concerned not only with improving the fabric, appearance and facilities of the city, but also with making it increasingly attractive to visitors.

None of this is really surprising to Glaswegians who have regained their old confidence in their city. It does, after all, have more than 60 public parks, some of them hundreds of acres in extent. Moreover, a city which is the base for Scottish Opera, Scottish Ballet and the Scottish National Orchestra – as well as having innumerable individuals and organizations involved in smaller musical, theatrical and artistic activities – is certainly not afraid to contemplate any large-scale cultural enterprise.

The one event above all others which put Glasgow in its new outgoing and confident mood was the opening of the Burrell Gallery in Pollok Country Park. As long ago as 1944 the city had been presented with the remarkable 8000-piece art collection gathered over many decades by the shipowner Sir William Burrell.

However, the conditions attached to the construction and location of a building to house it were not satisfied until the present gallery was completed in 1983.

The Burrell Collection's ceramics, jades, bronzes, stained glass, carpets and tapestries, silver and glassware, paintings, furniture and furnishings are displayed in an imaginative modern building which has such extensive areas of glass outer walls that the lawns and woodlands of the park seem almost part of the collection.

Elsewhere in the park, Pollok House is a handsome Palladian mansion and a museum in its own right, with notable furniture, plasterwork and Spanish paintings. Just outside the boundaries of Pollok Country Park, which also includes woodland and riverbank trails and a countryside visitor centre, Haggs Castle museum is devoted to the interests and activities of children.

At Kelvingrove, Glasgow's principal Art Gallery and Museum stands in another riverside park. The city's art collection, even before the Burrell acquisition, was probably the finest municipally owned one in Britain.

The idea of having museums in parks is by no means a new one in Glasgow. Glasgow Green is regarded locally as the oldest city-centre public park in Europe. It was acquired by the town council as far back as 1662,

The busy Victoria Bridge across the Clyde in Glasgow was built in 1851–54 on the site of a medieval river crossing

but had been a place of guaranteed public access for hundreds of years before that.

In the heart of the Green the late-Victorian People's Palace contains a museum crammed with items, concentrating on Glasgow's industries, personalities and rampaging old-style political life. Attached to it is a tall, flamboyant conservatory called the Winter Gardens, recently completely rebuilt at a cost of over £700,000.

Converted to serve as Britain's top indoor-sports centre, the Kelvin Hall also houses the Museum of Transport's extensive collections of Scottish-built motor cars, Glasgow trams and ship models.

All the museums, galleries and parks mentioned so far are publicly owned.

Charles Rennie Mackintosh was the most famous exponent, in architecture and furnishing design, of the turn-of-the-century 'Glasgow style'. His work is seen at its best in buildings like the Art School, Scotland Street School and Queens Cross Church, and in the painstaking reconstruction, within the tower of the Hunterian Art Gallery at Glasgow University, of the interior of his own house, which was nearby.

There are many other worthwhile buildings designed by architects working at the height of Glasgow's 19th-century prosperity, like the gracefully curving Park Terrace on the skyline of Kelvingrove Park, the terraces along Great Western Road near the Botanic Gardens, and the substantial office buildings which line St Vincent Street.

Nothing, however, displays to better advantage the confidence of Victorian Glasgow than its City Chambers. Guided tours of the building point out lavish

The Burrell Collection is one of the most important in Britain, covering a wide range of antiquities and art, with subject areas devoted to the ancient world, Oriental art, European decorative art, and other aspects. This is the courtyard of the museum building in Pollok Country Park

interior marble and alabaster work, ornate ceilings and satinwood-panelled walls.

By far the oldest building in the city is its cathedral, a work of medieval detail and proportions, which is constantly maintained and given appropriate modern additions to the furnishings of its individual chapels.

In 1987 work started to rebuild the square in front of the cathedral and provide an interpretation centre. Some distance away, a brand-new concert hall will, it is hoped, be open in time for the Culture Year of 1990. The Glasgow stretch of the long-disused Forth and Clyde Canal is being restored, with new pubs and restaurants along the 12 miles of waterway due to be reopened to leisure navigation by the autumn of 1989.

Close to the central George Square, an area designated the Merchant City has been redeveloped to the point where there are almost certainly more people living in it than at any time this century. The historic Ramshorn Kirk may become a centre for traditional music and it is planned that the redundant Sheriff Court building should be transformed into a major fashion complex, with workshops, displays and designers' studios.

In the next few years, half a dozen new ideas will have come to fruition; it is virtually impossible for anyone writing about the city to keep pace with its remarkable new developments.

Loch Lomond and Loch Awe

BEFORE THE CURRENT REJUVENATION of the city be-gan, Glasgow used to pride itself, only half ironically, as being 'a great place to get out of'. Loch Lomond has always been within easy reach – nowadays, for example, by way of the M8 motorway, the Erskine Bridge, Dumbarton and the high-level Vale of Leven bypass on the A82, which gives hints of the glorious mountain scenery ahead.

Just off the A82, **Balloch** is where the River Leven flows from Loch Lomond on its short journey to the Clyde. Several boatyards offer cruises round the southern end of the loch, while Balloch Pier is the starting point for the head-of-the-loch cruises in the larger *Countess Fiona*. Balloch Castle Country Park features woodland trails, a visitor centre, a walled garden and spacious picnic lawns overlooking the loch. In summer, yachts, cruisers, dinghies and canoes pass leisurely by.

As it follows the west side of Loch Lomond, the A82 is still only partway through a massive modernization programme. **Luss** is a Victorian estate village familiar to television viewers as 'Glendarroch' in the series *Take the High Road*, with a lochside pier, a parish church on historic ground above the loch, splendid views of a cluster of wooded islands and Ben Lomond

rising in the distance from the forested eastern shore.

Only a hamlet in size, Inverbeg manages to pack in an old coaching hotel, an art gallery, an unobtrusive lochside harbour and a youth hostel set in the deeply wooded ravine of the Douglas Water. Here, Loch Lomond has already narrowed dramatically and the mountains now crowd in.

Tarbet is bigger and at a road-junction, with boating facilities and cruises. Beyond it, on the increasingly winding A82, **Inveruglas** is a scattered settlement from which hill-walkers and climbers make for the cluster of 3000-ft (900-m) peaks in the 'Arrochar Alps'. A roadside hydroelectric power station is fed by the waters of the high-level Loch Sloy.

Right at the head of Loch Lomond, **Ardlui** is another small holiday and boating resort, with a station on the scenic West Highland Railway. Now the route begins to climb Glen Falloch, passing the Falls of Falloch which crash into a hidden rocky pool.

Up on the high ground, the A82 reaches mountain-fringed **Crianlarich**, where it turns west along Strath

A view of Ben Lomond (3192 ft, 974 m) from Inveruglas on the west side of Loch Lomond, showing the wooded hillside where the West Highland Way runs above the eastern shore

Fillan. Walking parties are often encountered here, tramping the West Highland Way.

Tyndrum has turned itself into a busy stopping-place for tourists. Interestingly enough, while there is still the debris of long-abandoned lead workings on one of the hillsides, a mining company has just signed an agreement to start large-scale prospecting for gold.

Out of Tyndrum, the route bears left along the A85 through Glen Lochy, cutting between the mountains towards **Dalmally**, a line also followed by the Oban branch of the West Highland Railway. In Dalmally, a side road leads to Monument Hill where, from the memorial rotunda to the Gaelic poet Duncan Ban MacIntyre, there is a superb panorama over the massif of Ben Cruachan, the twin arms at the north end of Loch Awe and the wooded islands which scatter their watery junction.

Beyond Dalmally the route turns left on to the A819, but not far away, beside the continuation of the A85, there is a car park for visitors to the ruined Campbell stronghold of Kilchurn Castle. From the pier beside the railway station at Lochawe village summer cruises round the islands are run by the steam launch *Lady Rowena*.

Back on route, the A819 swings along beside Loch Awe before heading over the hills to **Inveraray**, the very attractive Georgian town on the shore of the salt-water Loch Fyne. Inveraray Castle, open to visitors, is

Seat of the Dukes of Argyll, Inveraray Castle was built in a neo-gothic style in the 18th Century, and complements the neat little town of white-walled buildings beside Loch Fyne

the impressive home of the Duke of Argyll, head of Clan Campbell. In its grounds a Combined Services Museum recalls the hectic times in World War II when Inveraray was a major training base for tens of thousands of commandos and assault troops.

From Inveraray the A83 is a well-engineered and pleasantly wooded road round the head of Loch Fyne. A minor deviation through the village of Cairndow leads to Strone Woodland Garden, where a Grand Fir at over 200 ft (60 m) is the tallest tree in Britain.

A right turn on to the A815 and then a left turn on to the narrow and winding B839 lead into a landscape far different from the open lochside – Hell's Glen, where heavily forested hillsides close in.

Turning left on to the B828 the route comes into more open country again as it scrambles up another glen to rejoin the A83 at the top of the Rest and be Thankful. The modern road down past the rugged mountainsides takes an easier line than its predecessor seen far below.

Glen Croe runs along the edge of the Argyll Forest Park, and there are many waymarked hill and forest walks off to the south. Beyond Ardgartan the road swings round the head of Loch Long to **Arrochar**, from which there is a clear view westwards to the curious summit rock formation which gives Ben Arthur its more popular alternative name of The Cobbler.

At Arrochar the route turns on to the A814 which, as it runs along the wooded eastern shore of Loch Long, hardly deserves the classification. It is a narrow and twisting road with innumerable brows.

Climbing over a narrow neck of land, with a magnificent view, over to the right, of the mountainous, fjord-like meeting of Loch Goil and Loch Long, the route descends again to follow the east bank of the Gare Loch, into the residential town and sailing centre of **Helensburgh**.

This was the birthplace in 1888 of the television pioneer John Logie Baird, although the tall monument on the seafront is to Henry Bell, provost of the town and designer of the world's first seagoing steamship, the little *Comet*, launched in 1812. The National Trust for Scotland's property Hill House, at the top level of this hillside town, was one of the major commissions of the architect Charles Rennie Mackintosh.

Passing the side road leading to the walks round the nature reserve peninsula of Ardmore, the A814 returns to **Dumbarton** and two highly contrasting places of interest. The Denny Experiment Tank, open on occasion to visitors, is the long artificial-wave channel where Dumbarton's most famous firm of shipbuilders tested new designs in model form.

The ancient monument of Dumbarton Castle occupies the old volcanic Dumbarton Rock. Stairways and footpaths to its twin summits open up spectacular panoramic views, and there are gun platforms, a powder magazine and a prison as reminders that this was once a very businesslike fortress indeed.

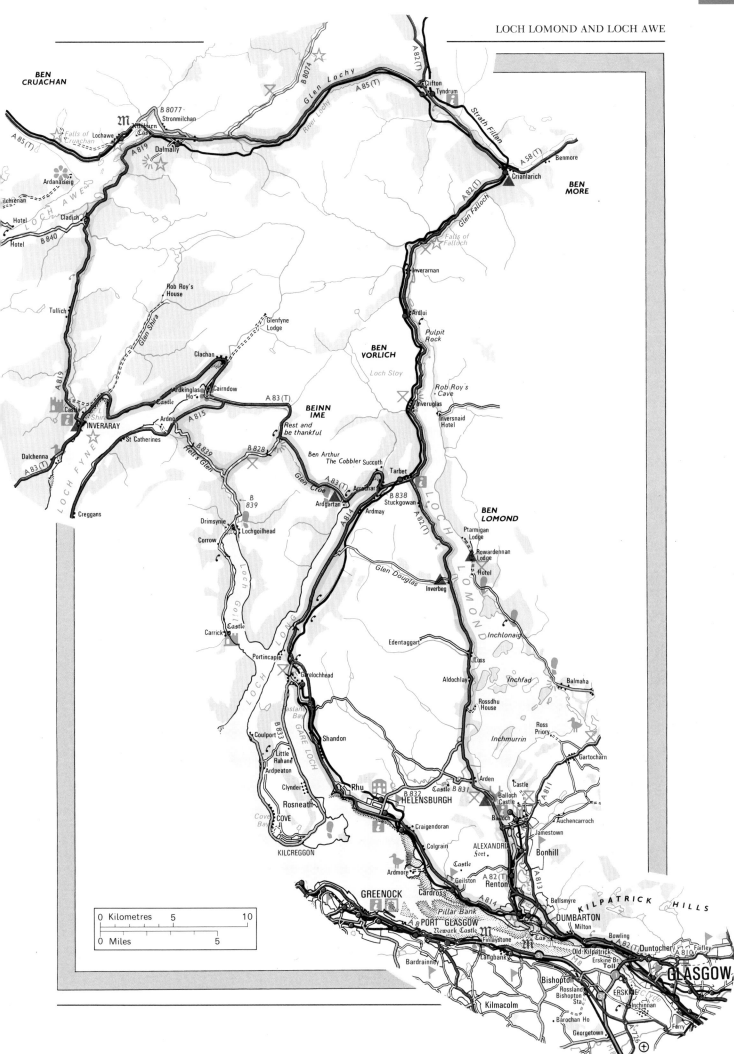

Glen Coe and Fort William

THIS TOUR begins at Bridge of Orchy and heads north to the Black Mount and Glen Coe, through some of the most open landscape in Scotland, with miles of mysterious moorland and almost overwhelming mountain views.

Bridge of Orchy is a hamlet with a former coaching hotel and a railway station on the Fort William line. The present A82 was built in the 1930s, but a short stretch of the old road still exists as the A8005, running alongside the rapids of the River Orchy, past the lonely and historic inn at Inveroran to Forest Lodge; beyond that point it is no longer tarred and open only to walkers.

From Bridge of Orchy the A82 goes into a long, steady climb before dipping down towards **Loch Tulla** and then swinging sharply up again on the climb of the Black Mount. It descends once more to pass the chilly and boulder-strewn waters of a wilder roadside loch which drains north-eastwards into the bare, deserted country of **Rannoch Moor**. This trackless expanse of peat mosses, open water and sluggish burns is not a moor in any conventional upland sense. To the left there is a dramatic view towards the peaks and corries of the Black Mount deer forest.

Another climb and gradual descent guide the road towards **Glen Coe**. Buachaille Etive Mor – the Great Shepherd of Etive – guards the entrance to the glen. This famous rock-climbers' playground is one of the most perfectly proportioned mountains in the whole of Scotland.

Before it, a short side road turns left to the White Corries ski-lift. To the right stands the isolated King's House Hotel, originally a staging post on a military road of the 1750s. On the left again, another side road

High peaks flank the Glen Coe road running west towards Ballachulish. Bidean nam Bian is prominent on the left, and the ridge Aonach Eagach is on the right.

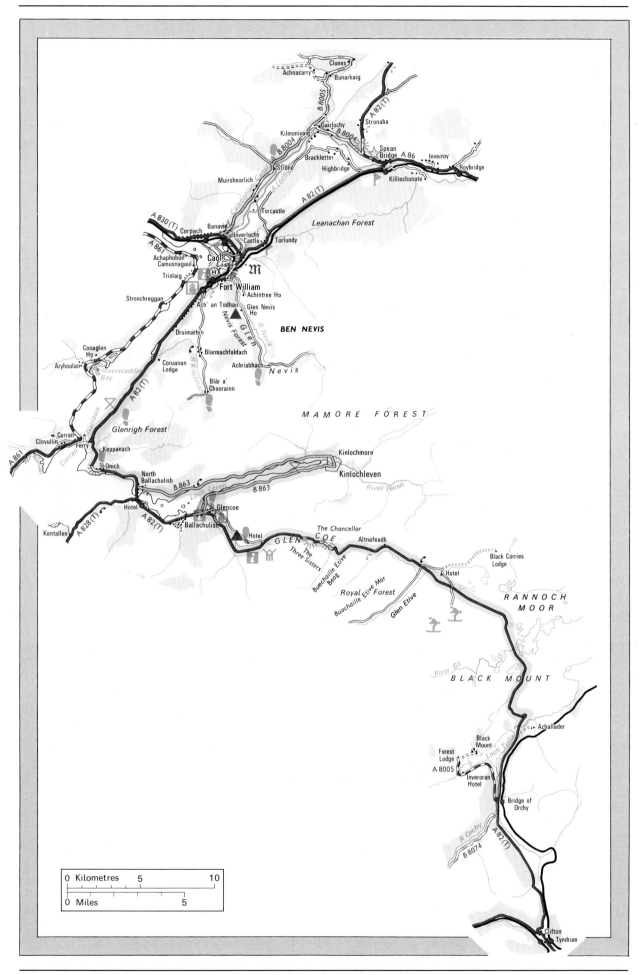

slinks below soaring mountainsides to the head of Loch Etive which, although far inland, is actually an arm of the sea.

Going straight on down Glen Coe, the A82 is hemmed in by mountains which loom up eerily out of mist or cloud. As they face the glen, all the south-side buttresses and steep subsidiary valleys from the Buachaille Etive Mor onwards, and the towering north-side ridge beyond Altnafeadh, are on a 14,000-acre (5600 ha) National Trust for Scotland estate.

The Trust has an excellent visitor centre in the lower part of the glen, with displays on geology, wildlife and rock-climbing, and also on that 17th-century act of savagery when government troops billeted on the local MacDonald families were secretly ordered, at dead of night, to slaughter their unsuspecting hosts.

Down near the shore of **Loch Leven**, just off the A82, **Glencoe** village has a folk museum, a memorial to the massacre of 1692 and an enjoyable forest walk round a lochan fringed with rhododendrons and Corsican pine.

Although the direct road to Fort William is the A82 across the Ballachulish bridge, the route turns away along the old main road, now numbered B863, which runs high above the south side of Loch Leven to **Kinlochleven**, the little industrial town at its head.

Kinlochleven is dominated by a ring of mountains. The possibility of building high-level reservoirs to feed a hydroelectric power station attracted an aluminium

factory here early this century. It is still the town's major employer. Walks based on Kinlochleven vary from riverside strolls to the steep mountain pathways which are part of the West Highland Way.

Along the north side of the loch, the route follows a much lower line towards **North Ballachulish** and then rejoins the A82 as it heads towards Fort William.

In **Fort William** there are displays of great historical interest in the West Highland Museum, and the Ben Nevis Exhibition tells the story of Britain's highest mountain. A side road in the town heads up Glen Nevis, finishing at a car park from which keen walkers can tackle a footpath into the magnificent Nevis Gorge.

From **Spean Bridge** the A82 climbs to the dramatic

The Commando Memorial stands on a viewpoint near Spean Bridge, overlooking the rugged country that was a Commando training area during the Second World War

Commando Memorial raised in honour of the men, trained in these great Lochaber hills and glens, who lost their lives in World War II.

At the memorial, a left turn on to the B8004 leads to Gairlochy and Banavie on a loop back towards Fort William. **Gairlochy** is a hamlet with two locks and a swing bridge over the Caledonian Canal. The route beyond it runs below forestry plantations and opens up a spectacular view across the valley to Ben Nevis, at last seen standing proud of its foothills.

Neptune's Staircase, the flight of eight locks at **Banavie** which lifts the canal from sea-level to the summit stretch extending all the way to Gairlochy, is one of Scotland's most impressive monuments to Thomas Telford's inspired work in civil engineering.

Buttresses and gullies emerging from clouds on the north face of Ben Nevis, Britain's highest mountain. In the foreground is the Charles Inglis Clark memorial hut – the only purpose-built 'Alpine' climbing hut in Scotland – it belongs to the Scottish Mountaineering Club

Kinross and Strath Tay

SCOTLAND'S TWO **LOCH LEVENS** could hardly be more different. The West Highland sea-loch is a fjord flanked by uninterrupted mountains. The inland loch, which formed a substantial part of the old county of Kinross-shire, is dotted with islands and is surrounded for the most part by level farmland, although the hills which rise to east and south create up-draughts of wind which make this Scotland's premier gliding area.

Kinross is a fine old county town, whose principal hotels used to be rivals for the coaching trade. It is the base for the fleet of boats which take anglers on to the loch's famous trout waters. A passenger ferry operates to the wooded island whose castle was the prison where Mary Queen of Scots was held for many months as courtiers tried to force her abdication, and from which she made the dramatic escape which was one of the most exciting episodes in an adventurous life.

Loch Leven is also a National Nature Reserve which attracts thousands of wintering geese as well as having a large resident bird population. The RSPB's Vane Farm nature centre, lying back from the southern shore, is the main information and observation point.

Leaving Kinross to the west, the route passes the massive white 'golf ball' of a radio communications station on the wartime Balado airfield before following the A91 along the foot of the Ochils. Then it turns on to the A823, which cuts across these rounded and often forested hills. Up narrow **Glen Devon** and down narrow **Glen Eagles**, the road follows the line of an old cattle-drovers' route, along which herds from the Highlands were walked to the great livestock market at Falkirk.

Back on lower ground, **Gleneagles Hotel** is an imposing baronial affair surrounded by four golf courses on its own estate. It was opened after World War 1 by the London, Midland and Scottish Railway. Despite several recent changes of ownership, it retains its fine international reputation.

To the right of the A823 as it heads north, signs indicate the way to places of interest along the minor roads to the right: the handsomely restored 15th-century Tullibardine Chapel, now an ancient monument; and the Strathallan Museum Park, which has added cars and a great variety of transport models to its original collection of full-size aircraft.

After a turn on to the A822, **Muthill** (pronounced 'Myooth'll') is a village on the main road, which repays much closer attention than passing motorists often give

Outside Pitlochry this dam holds the waters of Loch Faskally. Its fish ladder (on the left) allows salmon to make their way to spawning grounds higher up the River Tummel

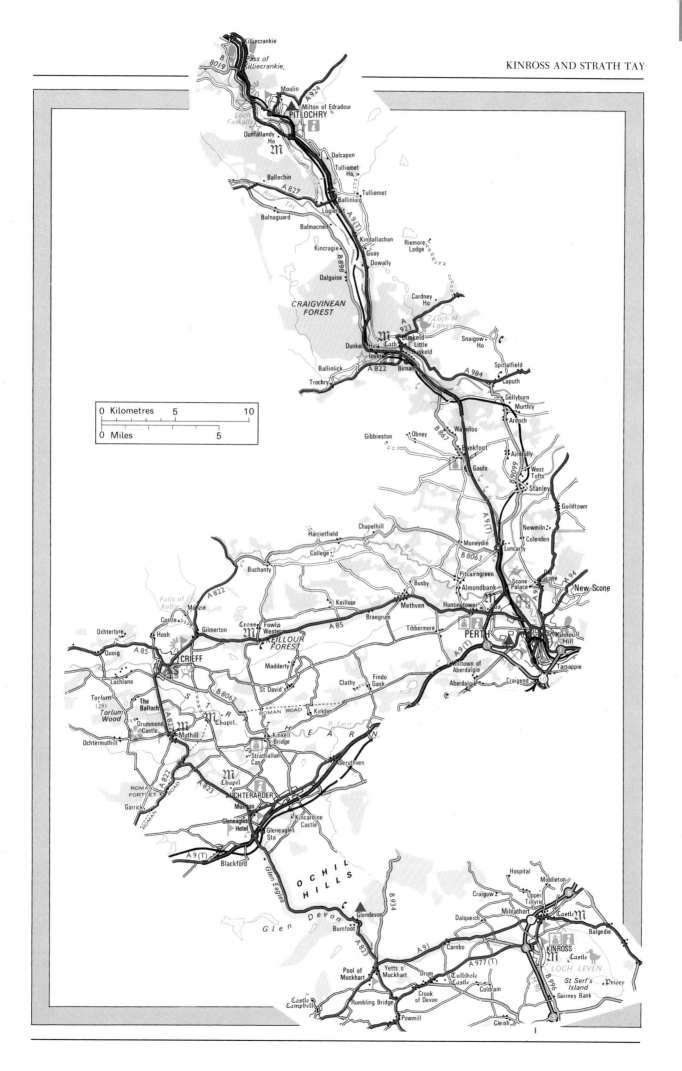

it. Once an overnight stopping place on the great cattle drives which also used Glen Eagles and Glen Devon, it has sturdy 18th-century houses, traces of the Roman occupation in its neighbourhood, and the Romanesque tower of a medieval parish church preserved as an ancient monument.

North-west of Muthill, Drummond Castle boasts some of the most elegant formal gardens in Scotland. Farther on, the A822 reaches **Crieff**, a busy hillside town which offers guided tours of glass-blowing and pottery workshops and, at the nearby hamlet called the Hosh, of Glenturret malt whisky distillery, the oldest in Scotland. There are fine walks on the wooded Knock of Crieff, the hill which overlooks the town and the spreading plain of Strathearn and, as the route leaves

Crieff for Gilmerton, it passes a hillside golf course.

From **Gilmerton** the A85 heads directly for Perth. Fowlis Wester, on a side road to the left, is a pleasant little village with an intricately carved Pictish cross and a restored pre-Reformation church which retains its 'leper squint'.

Nearer Perth, the ancient monument of Hunting-tower Castle has features of the 15th, 16th and 17th centuries, with particularly fine painted ceilings. It was the home of the Ruthvens until they became so disastrously embroiled in the politics of James VI's reign – to the extent of kidnapping the young king and holding him prisoner here – that even their very name was outlawed.

Perth is one of most attractively situated major

towns in Scotland, built on both banks of the River Tay, with a magnificent public park on the wooded Kinnoull Hill high above. St John's Kirk in the town centre is where John Knox preached the robust sermon which lit the fires of Reformation in Scotland. Balhousie Castle is the fascinating museum of the Black Watch regiment. There are museums and galleries, tours of a paperweight factory and a distillery, angling on the town stretch of the Tay and several golf courses – one of them on a river island.

North of Perth the modernized A9 bypasses all the towns and villages to Pitlochry, but visiting them involves only minor detours. At **Bankfoot** the Highland Motor Heritage Centre restores vintage and historic cars and keeps several on display.

A **Westland Lysander** of the early 1940s in the Strathallan Museum Park, off the B8062 near Auchterarder. The Strathallan Collection includes aircraft and cars, and models of other types of transport

Birnam is full of mid-Victorian houses and has beautiful hill, woodland and riverside walks. One of them passes the ancient, propped-up oak tree, which is claimed to be the last remnant of the Birnam Wood in *Macbeth*. Across the Tay from the Terrace Walk, Eastwood is the isolated house where Beatrix Potter wrote the picture letters later expanded into the tales of Peter Rabbit and Mr Jeremy Fisher the frog.

Dunkeld is a cathedral city – of the size of a small town – which was once the ecclesiastical centre of the Scottish kingdom. The partly ruined cathedral, on a lovely site above the Tay, is still in use as the parish church. A street of 18th-century houses, neatly restored by the National Trust for Scotland, leads towards it, and there is a good information centre. In the square by the cathedral stands the regimental museum of the Scottish Horse.

Like Birnam, Dunkeld is the centre for some fine woodland walks, and there are still more to the left of the A9 beyond it, in Craigvinean Forest. Craigvinean's plantations rise to the summit of a lofty ridge and surround a National Trust for Scotland property, the Hermitage, an 18th-century summerhouse and folly above the romantic falls of the Braan.

The route ends at **Pitlochry**, a holiday resort set among hills and forests, on the banks of the River Tummel. The river was dammed as part of a massive hydroelectric scheme, creating not a dull-looking reservoir but the beautiful Loch Faskally, winding between wooded banks. A visitor centre at the dam explains the workings of the scheme, and has windows looking into the salmon pass, through which the fish are still able to struggle up to their spawning grounds.

The town is a golfing, angling, hill-walking and pony-trekking centre, with facilities for all kinds of open-air activities, but it is also the location of the famous Pitlochry Festival Theatre, founded in 1951 and now occupying a modern building by the river.

Loch Leven, east of Kinross, is famous for the Vane Farm reserve of the Royal Society for the Protection of Birds (in the foreground) and for its trout. A ferry runs from a lochside park at Kinross to Castle Island

Blairgowrie and Royal Deeside

BLAIRGOWRIE and its twin town Rattray face each other across the River Ericht, where that river, which rises in the Highlands, flows out of a narrow and winding glen on to the Stormont plain. As the fields around them show, this is the centre of the Scottish soft-fruit industry, with a flourishing export trade, especially in raspberries.

South of Blairgowrie, the members of the beautifully landscaped Rosemount Golf Club enjoy one of the finest inland layouts in Scotland. To the west, Ardblair Castle is a house with many Jacobite mementos. Occasional guided tours are arranged through the Blairgowrie tourist office.

Winding north up the Ericht valley, the A93 follows the line of an old military road into Glen Shee, where there are farmhouses in the narrow valley floor but increasingly wilder hills above. At **Spittal of Glenshee** the road begins to tackle the exhilarating climb of the Cairnwell Pass to the Glenshee skiing grounds. This is still often described as the Devil's Elbow, but that once forbidding hairpin near the summit has been bypassed

for several years, although the whole road is sometimes closed by drifting winter snows.

The Cairnwell summit, at almost 2200 ft (670 m), is the highest point on any main road in Britain. Beyond it the A93 stays in wild hill country for a while, before running down alongside the narrow fields in Glen Clunie to **Braemar**. This is a sturdy granite-built village, in one of whose houses Robert Louis Stevenson, during a family holiday in 1881, wrote most of *Treasure Island*.

People come here for angling, deer-stalking, grouse-shooting, hill-walking and climbing. Braemar's midwinter temperatures are often the lowest in Britain, but it has an invigorating summer air.

This is a place steeped in Jacobite history, where the Earl of Mar raised the standard to begin the Rising of 1715. However, the present royal family has nothing to

The Royal Family's private residence in Scotland, Balmoral Castle. It was built by Queen Victoria and Prince Albert on a bend in the River Dee in the 1850s

The Dee near Ballater, with the distant peaks of Lochnagar away to the south above Balmoral Forest. The area includes a major mountain reserve, run by Balmoral Estates and the Scottish Wildlife Trust

fear in what was once a Jacobite stronghold, not least because Queen Victoria first gave her patronage to the Braemar Highland Gathering in 1848, and that family interest has continued to the present day. Every September the gathering draws tens of thousands of spectators to a day of piping and dancing competitions, track and hill races, and 'heavy events' like the tossing of the massive Braemar caber.

As the A93 keeps right to follow the valley of the Dee, it passes Braemar Castle, open to visitors, which was once the home of the Earls of Mar, later a government barracks and is now owned by an old-established family, the Farquharsons of Invercauld.

The route enters the classic scenery of Royal Deeside, with pine trees overlooking the rocky banks of a sparkling river, and heathery hillsides above. A few miles after it crosses to the north bank at Invercauld Bridge, there are glimpses of the beautiful surroundings of **Balmoral Castle**, the royal family's private Scottish home.

The entrance to Balmoral is on the B976, after it crosses the river again. The same car park serves the castle and the little parish church of Crathie, where members of the royal family worship. Balmoral's lawn-and-woodland grounds are open to visitors only in May, June and July. Although the main part of the castle is not included, there is an art exhibition in the ballroom.

From Balmoral the B976 is the South Deeside road. John Begg operated the Lochnagar Distillery here in Victoria and Albert's day, and gained the Royal Warrant in 1848 after a hearty tasting session in which both the royal couple took part.

Off to the right of the B976, just before it reaches **Ballater**, side roads lead to Loch Muick (pronounced 'Mick'), which is surrounded by mountains and is the heart of a major nature reserve.

Ballater itself, on the north side of the Dee, is a fine little granite town, with many shops displaying the Royal Warrant. Its golf course occupies a curve of level riverside ground, and there are walks both along the riverbank and on the wooded local hills, the finest of them being on Craigendarroch – the Crag of the Oak Trees – which is ringed by good footpaths and has a superb view from the summit.

Beyond Ballater the route passes Pannanich Wells Hotel, site of the mineral spring whose healing waters attracted so many 18th-century invalids that Ballater was founded to accommodate their growing numbers.

Gliders can often be seen, launched from the airstrip near **Dinnet** on the north side of the Dee. Then the B976 arrives at the dramatic entrance lodge to Glen Tanar, beside the Bridge o'Ess. A side road turns off here towards the visitor centre in this lovely valley of pinewoods and waymarked trails.

The route finishes north of the Dee again at **Aboyne**, whose village green has since 1867 been the venue of the Aboyne Highland Games. But there is no sign now of the rafts of Glen Tanar pine and oak trees, which used to be lashed together here, then floated down river to the boatyards and timber merchants of Aberdeen.

The essence of **Grampian Mountains** scenery, as the Dee ripples down from the Forest of Mar towards Braemar

Speyside and Nairn

AVIEMORE is the main year-round holiday resort in the Spey Valley, dominated from the west by the birch-wood cliffs of the Craigellachie nature reserve. In the other direction, the huge bulk of the Cairngorms fills the south-eastern skyline. The route heads directly for them, crossing the River Spey past the whisky museum at **Inverdruie** and the visitor centre for the Rothiemurchus estate.

At **Coylumbridge** a right turn leads through stately pinewoods to Loch Morlich and the **Glen More Forest Park**. Guided tours can be arranged to the grazing areas of Scotland's only herd of reindeer, established from Lapland stock in the 1950s.

Bending south, the route beyond Glenmore becomes the 'ski road', climbing steadily above the forest to the high-level car parks which in winter and early spring serve the Cairngorm chair-lifts and ski-tows. The whole year round a chair-lift operates to the Ptarmigan Restaurant. At around 3600 ft (1100 m), this is the highest building in Britain, with correspondingly breathtaking views.

Back down at Coylumbridge, the route turns right on to the B970 past **Boat of Garten**, the base of the privately run Strathspey Railway, which operates steam-hauled trains to and from Aviemore. Beyond Boat of Garten – named after the ferry which once crossed the Spey here – a side road on the right leads through more pinewoods to the RSPB's **Loch Garten** reserve. Ospreys nest every year, and can be observed through binoculars from the well-equipped visitor centre.

Nethy Bridge is a holiday centre for angling, walking, pony-trekking and golf. Surprisingly, in the 18th century it was a hive of industry, supplying the boatyards at the mouth of the Spey with felled timber from the Abernethy pinewoods, floated down river in rafts.

Turning left on to the A95 and crossing the Spey again, the route enters **Grantown-on-Spey**, a much more traditional resort than Aviemore. It was originally laid out in the 18th century, but began to expand as Victorian doctors recommended its healthy air. Modern Grantown is noted for its salmon fishing and golf, soft-surfaced low-level pinewood walks, good granite buildings and neatly arranged square.

So far, the route has never been out of sight of pines, birchwoods or spruce plantations. As the A939 heads north from Grantown, however, it leads into a quite different landscape: the wide-open Dava Moor and the flurry of glacial lochans by the windings of the Dorback Burn.

A preserved London, Midland and Scottish Railway Pacific locomotive starts its train for Aviemore at Boat of Garten station on the Strathspey Railway

After several miles the forests begin again in the valley of the River Findhorn. On the left, after the Findhorn bridge, a side road leads to **Ardclach**, where the parish church was set so low by the river bank that in 1655 a separate bell-tower (now an ancient monument) was built high above it, otherwise the sound of the bell – which acted both as a call to worship and as a warning of attack – would never have carried.

More forest and farming country leads to **Nairn**, an attractive county town and holiday resort with long beaches, excellent golf courses, riverside walks, a good heritage trail and a local museum in the once appropriately named Fishertown.

Turning south-west on the B9091, the route reaches the crossroads at **Clephanton**, where a short diversion left leads to **Cawdor** and its impressive castle, named in *Macbeth*, although the present building was begun centuries after the action of the play. Cawdor Castle and its gardens are open to the public, and so are miles of fascinating nature trails in the woodlands crossed by two tumbling Highland burns.

Continuing south-west from Clephanton, the B9091 joins the B9006 at **Croy** and makes for the site of the Battle of Culloden, fought in 1746. The National Trust for Scotland has the battlefield in its care, and mounts several displays – about the fighting at this sombre and

atmospheric place, about the origins of the Jacobite movement and about the aftermath of the battle, when the old Highland way of life was destroyed for ever. Jacobite clansmen killed in the battle lie in their own clan graves.

Retracing its steps from the battlefield, the route turns right on to the B851, although a loop-shaped minor road across to the south-east side of the River Nairn gives access to the famous Clava group of Neolithic chambered burial cairns.

Turning on to the A9 the route leads past **Daviot** and its striking parish church, alongside the Inverness-Perth railway in the rugged defile of the Slochd summit, and then to the side road for **Carrbridge** on the River Dulnain. The stone bridge which gave the village its name in 1717 survives as a single, elegant high-arched span. The imaginative Landmark Centre includes audio-visual and other displays on Highland history and wildlife, a boardwalk maze and even – securely raised on timber stilts – a treetop-level pinewood trail.

Beyond Carrbridge the Cairngorms and their forested foothills are once again more clearly in focus.

A 'tower house' castle built in the late 14th Century, Cawdor is famous in legend – if not in historical fact – as the home of Macbeth. Buildings around the core are later additions

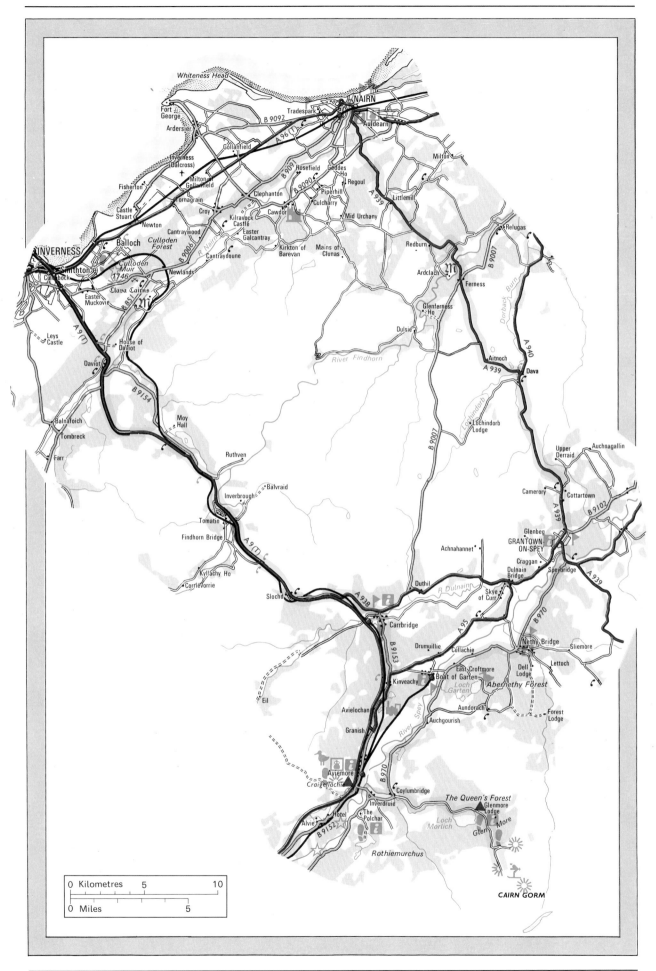

Loch Ness

INVERNESS is the transport, trading, shopping and administrative centre of the vast Highland Region. The River Ness flows briskly through on its way to the Moray Firth, and many of the town's most notable features are clustered round it. The highset 19th-century castle, a fine red-sandstone building which serves as a courthouse and council offices, provides an attractive viewpoint over the river and the forested hills beyond. Close by, there is a well-stocked local museum and art gallery. The modern Eden Court Theatre is on the far bank, and paths on both sides of the river are linked by footbridges to the wooded Ness Islands.

The route takes the A82 south-west from Inverness, across the Caledonian Canal. Inverness is the base for several cruises and charters on the loch, and boats are usually to be seen on the stretch of canal after the locks at Dochgarroch.

For some miles the A82 hugs the lochside until it turns away to curve through the villages of **Drumnadrochit** and **Lewiston**. The Loch Ness Monster Centre at Drumnadrochit displays photographs, drawings, sonar scans and examples of pure speculation concerning that world-famous phenomenon. It also gives details of expeditions which have come here from as far away as Japan. A side road in Lewiston ascends in hairpin bends towards the short oakwood walk to the Falls of Divach.

At **Strone**, where the A82 rejoins the lochside,

Left: the Caledonian Canal links Loch Ness to Lochs Oich, Lochy and eventually Loch Linnhe and the sea. It leaves the southern end of Loch Ness through these locks at Fort Augustus.
Right: a view south along Loch Ness, from outside Fort Augustus

Urquhart Castle is a ruined but finely situated ancient monument. Not far beyond it is the memorial to John Cobb, the land speed record holder who was killed on Loch Ness in 1952, trying to add the water speed record in his jet-engined boat *Crusader*.

The A82 is a very pleasant road on this part of the lochside, with steep Forestry Commission spruce plantations on the right and a fringe of birch, rowan and alder woodland on the left.

Most motorists simply drive through **Invermoriston**, the village where the A82 loops briefly 'inland' again to cross the River Moriston by a comparatively modern bridge. But it is well worth stopping here to admire the original bridge among the rock ledges down to the right, and to take a short stroll through the woodland on the left towards an old summerhouse overlooking falls and a sheer-sided gorge.

Passing the side road on the right towards the forest and riverside walks at Auchteraw, the A82 arrives in **Fort Augustus** at the head of Loch Ness. The flight of locks here lift the Caledonian Canal from the loch up to the next summit level southwards. Close at hand, the Great Glen Exhibition illustrates the story of the canal and of the long-vanished Invergarry and Fort Augustus Railway, which closed in 1910 and is regarded by affectionate railway historians as a purpose-built lost cause. Other exhibits concentrate on general history, clans and notable battles.

St Benedict's Abbey, open to visitors, is in beautiful surroundings on the edge of the village. Its dignified appearance hides the fact that several of its buildings began life as part of a Hanoverian fort, still on the site when it was given to the Benedictines in 1876.

Beside the entrance to the abbey grounds, the route bears left on the B862, beginning a climb above the east side of Loch Ness, which is soon lost to view as the road heads for the forested valley of Stratherrick. After Whitebridge a left turn on to the B852 leads along a winding birch-edged road to the hillside village of **Foyers**, which was chosen in the 1890s as the location of Britain's first aluminium factory.

The main attraction was the possibility of tapping the Falls of Foyers for hydroelectric power. Although the aluminium works closed in 1967, the falls have never regained their full original flow. Woodland paths reveal the still spectacular ravine, down which the now restricted flow careers into dark rock pools.

Beyond Foyers, the road follows a fairly high-level line above Loch Ness. It dips down at **Inverfarigaig**, where a side road to the right immediately before the River Farigaig bridge takes the route into a precipitous and darkly wooded gorge. Forest trails from a visitor centre climb through deciduous woodlands and spruce plantations to some dramatic viewpoints.

A sharp left turn over a bridge in the gorge takes the route to Errogie. The B862 and the B851 through the valley of Strathnairn lead on to the A9, which crests the final rise before Inverness to reveal a panoramic view of the fine situation of the town, the Beauly and Moray Firths, the farms and forests of the Black Isle, and the outlines of much grander mountains on the horizon.

Opposite: **Autumn colours** tint the shores of Loch Ness
Below: **Urquhart Castle** on the western shore of the loch

Skye

ALTHOUGH there has been pressure for a bridge to be built across the narrow strait from Kyle of Lochalsh to **Kyleakin**, the car ferry there remains the quickest way of reaching Skye. This island of magnificent mountain peaks and long, green peninsulas, which give it hundreds of miles of often cliff-bound coast, has a well-engineered main-road network.

From Kyleakin the route starts along the A850. About seven miles on, it passes the A851 turn-off for **Armadale** and the fascinating Clan Donald Centre.

The first major village on the route is **Broadford**, set back from a wide bay with fine views out to smaller islands and the mainland hills of Applecross. Broadford Hotel, overlooked by the green grassy cone of Beinn na Caillich, stands on the site of the inn where Prince Charles Edward Stuart, a fugitive on Skye after the Battle of Culloden, shared the secret recipe for his favourite liqueur with some MacKinnons, whose territory this was. Their descendants still market it today as Drambuie.

Broadford has facilities for angling, boating and hill-walking, and private postage stamps for the low-lying offshore island of Pabay are on sale. Farther on, a forest and coastal trail starts near a bay facing the higher, privately owned island of Scalpay.

The narrow channel between Scalpay and the mainland of Skye is a sensible location for a sailing and windsurfing centre, and there is pony-trekking here too. Past **Dunan** and the craft workshop which concentrates on local marble, the road swings above Loch Ainort to **Luib**.

Luib Folk Museum takes as its theme the crofting life of Skye early this century. Skye still has hundreds of crofts – smallholdings which usually have some arable land, a share of the hill grazings and the use of communally held peat banks where fuel can be cut free, except for the energetic labour involved.

West of the short pass from the head of **Loch Ainort**, **Glamaig** is a wilder hill than any seen close up before, rising steeply from rough heather moorland but giving only an indication of the scale of the mountain scenery to come.

On the far side of the pass, **Sconser** on Loch Sligachan has Skye's only (9-hole) golf course. A car ferry leaves for the smaller island of Raasay, with its hills, forests, moorlands, exhilarating walks and abundant remains of abandoned ironstone mines, worked for a time by German prisoners during World War I. Sligachan Hotel, beyond the head of the loch, is a

An inter-island ferry at Uig's pier, a focal point of this little village scattered around a sweeping bay

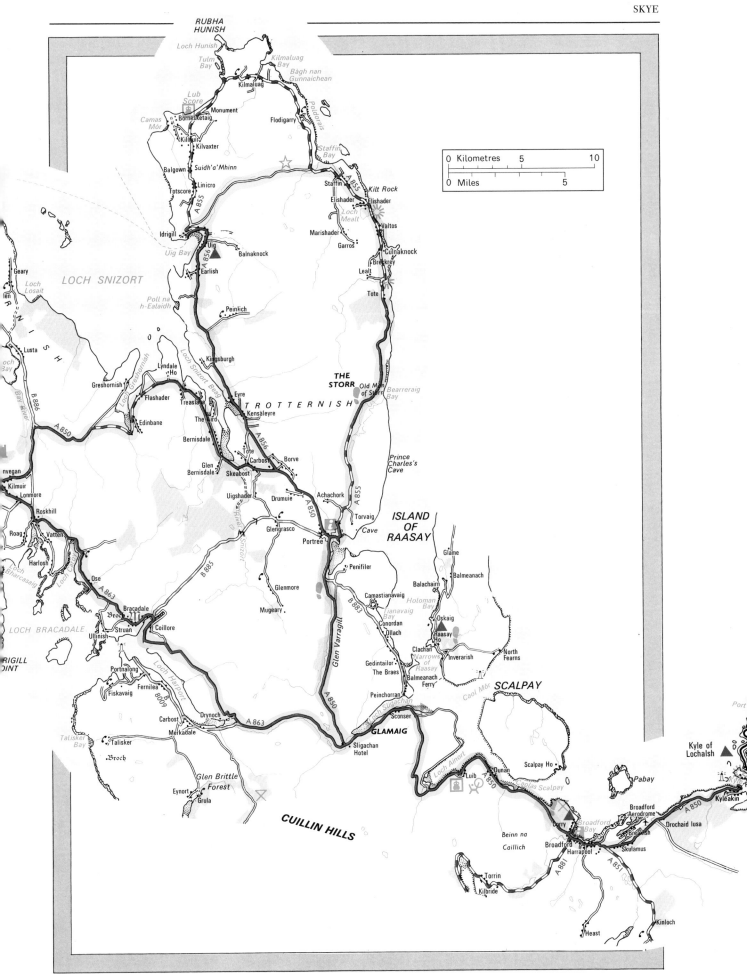

RUBHA HUNISH

Loch Hunish
Tulm Bay
Kilmaluag Bay
Bàgh nan Gunnaichean
Kilmaluag
Lub Score
Monument
Camas Mór
Bornesketaig
Flodigarry
Poldorais
Kilmuir
Kilvaxter
Staffin Bay
Balgown
Suidh'a'Mhinn
Staffin
Kilt Rock
Linicro
A 855
Elishader
Elishader
Totscore
Valtos
Loch Mealt
Idrigill
Marishader
Culnaknock
A 856
Uig
Garros
Breckrey
Uig Bay
Balnaknock
Lealt
Earlish
Tote
LOCH SNIZORT
Geary
Loch Losait
Poll na h-Ealaidh
Peinlich
Lusta
Kingsburgh
THE STORR
Bay
Lyndale Ho
Greshornish
Eyre
Old Man of Storr
Bearreraig Bay
B 886
Flashader
Treaslane
Kensaleyre
T R O T T E R N I S H
A 850
Edinbane
The Bird
Bernisdale
Tote
Borve
Prince Charles's Cave
A 856
Carbost
Invegan
Glen Bernisdale
Kilmuir
Skeabost
Lonmore
Uigshader
Drumuie
Achachork
Roskhill
Glengrasco
Torvaig
ISLAND OF RAASAY
Roag
Vatten
Portree
Cave
A 855
Harlosh
Penifiler
Glame
Loch Bharcasaig
Ose
A 863
Glenmore
Balachairn
Balmeanach
Bracadale
B 885
Camastianavaig
Broch
Tianavaig Bay
Holoman Bay
Struan
Coillore
Mugeary
B 883
Oskaig
LOCH BRACADALE
Ullinish
Conordan
Raasay Ho
Ollach
Clachan
RIGILL POINT
Portnalong
Loch Harport
Glen Varragil
Gedintailor
Narrows of Raasay
Inverarish
North Fearns
Fernilea
The Braes
Fiskavaig
B 8009
Balmeanach Ferry
SCALPAY
Drynoch
Peinchorran
Caol Mòr
Carbost
A 863
River Snizort
Sconser
Port C
Merkadale
Loch Sligachan
Talisker Bay
Glamaig
Kyle of Lochalsh
Talisker
Sligachan Hotel
Loch Ainort
Pabay
Broch
Dunan
Scalpay Ho
Skye Fer
Glen Brittle Forest
Luib
A 850
Kyleakin
Eynort
Grula
Caol Scalpay
Broadford Aerodrome
Drochaid lusa
Dorry
Broadford Bay
Breakish
CUILLIN HILLS
Beinn na Caillich
Broadford
Skulamus
A 881
Harrapool
A 851
Torrin
Kilbride
Heast
Kinloch

famous rock-climbers' base. The serrated Cuillin Ridge – with 16 peaks above 3000 ft (900 m) – dominates the southern horizon.

At **Sligachan** the route turns on to the A863, now a well-surfaced and well-graded road. However, in the pioneering days of motoring on Skye part of the Sligachan-Dunvegan-Portree-Sligachan circuit was on such narrow tracks that the few local drivers agreed to make it a huge, if unofficial, one-way system.

Passing the side road to Skye's only malt whisky distillery, Talisker, at Carbost, the route climbs the hills again to run high above **Loch Bracadale**, the great sea-bay dotted with islands where the chastened Viking fleet gathered in 1263 after its defeat at the Battle of Largs.

Passing more peninsulas and inlets, the route comes to **Dunvegan** and, beyond it, to the most famous building in Skye. For seven centuries, Dunvegan Castle has been the home of the MacLeods of MacLeod, and among the thousands of visitors who come here every year there are many MacLeods – often from abroad – keen to see the chief's residence.

From the road the approach to the castle is through woodlands and gardens; seen from the other side, it stands on a rugged sea-loch cliff. Public rooms in the castle tell the story of the MacLeods, and the remaining fragment of the 'fairy flag' which traditionally brought them good fortune is carefully preserved. There is also a small display on the Atlantic island group of St Kilda, whose rock stacks were once part of the MacLeod estates.

From Dunvegan the route takes the A850 by **Loch Greshornish** and over the River Snizort (the longest river on Skye, providing trout and salmon fishing) to a left turn on to the A856 which follows the coast of the northern Trotternish peninsula to Uig.

Uig has a fishing harbour and is a car ferry port for the Western Isles, with services to Tarbert in Harris and Lochmaddy in North Uist. The bay is overlooked from the north by a green hillside dotted with whitewashed houses, and the village itself is unusually well wooded for this part of the island.

The hairpin climb out of Uig comes to a junction where the A855 continues round the north end of Skye, past **Kilmuir** with its cluster of thatched buildings which make up the Skye Cottage Museum, and the graveyard with a memorial in the shape of the Celtic cross to Flora Macdonald. She was the Jacobite heroine who – in the words of the song which recalls a most daring escapade – brought a disguised Bonnie Prince Charlie 'over the sea to Skye' from a hiding-place in the Western Isles.

The tour route, however, takes a minor road to the right at the junction above the Uig hairpin, and heads across the Trotternish peninsula to the **Quiraing** where ancient landslips and weathering have created a weird landscape of rock pinnacles, grass-topped 'tables' and screes. Walkers enjoy both the glorious high-level views and the possibility of finding tiny mountain flowers.

Turning right to rejoin the A855 at **Staffin**, the route comes to another curious landscape formation where **Loch Mealt**, to the right of the road, is the source of a 150-ft (45-m) river which flows under a bridge and then hurtles down a 170-ft (52-m) cascade to the sea. There is also a view north to the Kilt Rock, given its name because its light-and-dark banded structure seems patterned and pleated like a kilt.

Farther on, as there are marvellous views to the deserted island of Rona, Raasay and the mainland hills of Wester Ross, a forest walk climbs into another area of remarkable pinnacled scenery, around the 160 ft (48 m) **Old Man of Storr**.

There is a downward walk, too, on the staircase leading to the beach beside a hydroelectric power

station; but visitors who trot happily down tend to look thoughtful at the bottom as they realize there are more than 500 steps back up to the top. The roadside Storr Lochs are good trout-fishing waters.

Portree is the capital of Skye, and a major touring resort built round a harbour and bay sheltered from easterly gales by the bulk of Raasay. There are many hotels, boarding houses and craft shops, as well as shoreline, hill and clifftop walks. The local visitor information service is based on Meall House, the oldest building in the town. It once served as the jail,

and the tourist information officer works in the old condemned cell.

South of Portree, past the sometimes dampish forest walks above Glen Varragill, the A850 takes the route full circle at Sligachan, most appropriately in full view of the majestic Cuillin Hills.

Elgol, at the end of the narrow A881, has magnificent views of the Cuillin Hills, and away to the south sea views towards some of the Inner Hebrides – Rhum, Eigg and Canna

Motorways and Major Routes

Legend

ROADS ROUTES STRASSEN

The representation on this map of a road is no evidence of the existence of a right of way

M 1 — Motorway with service area, service area (limited access) and junction with junction number
Autoroute avec aire de service, aire de service (accès restreint) et échangeur avec son numéro
Autobahn mit Servicestation, Servicestation (mit begrenztem Zugang) und Anschlußstelle mit Nummer

M 62 — Motorway junction with limited interchange
Echangeur à possibilités d'intercirculation restreintes
Autobahnanschlußstelle mit begrenztem Richtungswechsel

M 40 — Motorway under construction
Autoroute en construction
Autobahn im Bau

A 1(T) Dual carriageway — Trunk road with service area
Route à grande circulation avec aire de service
Fernverkehrsstrasse mit Servicestation

A 15 Double chaussée — Main road with roundabout or multiple level junction
Route principale avec rond-point, sens giratoire ou échangeur
Hauptstrasse mit Kreisverkehr oder Anschlußstelle

B 4069 Zweibahnige Strasse — Secondary road / Route secondaire / Nebenstrasse

Road under construction / Route en construction / Strasse im Bau

Gradient 1 in 7 and steeper / Pente: 14% et plus / Steigungen: 14% und mehr

Toll — Toll / Péage / Strassenbenutzungsgebühr — Road tunnel / Tunnel routier / Strassentunnel

A 855   B 797 — Narrow road with passing places / Route étroite avec voies de dépassment / Enge Strasse mit Ausweichstelle bzw. Uberholstelle

Other tarred road   Other minor road / Autre route goudronnée   Autre route / Sonstige asphaltierte Strasse Sonstige Nebenstrasse

18   23 — Distances in miles between markers / Distances en miles les marques / Entfernungen in Meilen zwischen den Zeichen

Selected places of major traffic importance are known as Primary Route Destinations and are shown on this map thus DERBY. Distances and directions to such destinations are repeated on traffic signs (see inside back cover).

TOURIST INFORMATION RENSEIGNEMENTS TOURISTIQUES TOURISTIKINFORMATION

Abbey, Cathedral, Priory / Abbaye, Cathédrale Prieuré / Abtei, Kathedrale, Priorei

Aquarium / Aquarium / Aquarium

Camp site / Terrain de camping / Campingplatz

Caravan site / Terrain pour caravanes / Wohnwagenplatz

Castle / Château / Schloss

Cave / Caverne / Höhle

Country park / Parc naturel / Landschaftspark

Craft centre / Centre artisanal / Zentrum für Kunsthandwerk

Garden / Jardin / Garten

Golf course or links / Terrain de golf / Golfplatz

Historic house / Manoir, Palais / Historisches Gebäude

Information centre / Bureau de renseignements / Informationsbüro

Motor racing / Courses automobiles / Autorennen

Museum / Musée / Museum

Nature or forest trail / Sentier signalisé pour piétons / Natur-oder Waldlehrpfad

Nature reserve / Réserve naturelle / Naturschutzgebiet

Other tourist feature / Autre site intéressant / Sonstige Sehenswurdigkeit

Picnic site / Emplacement de pique-nique / Picknickplatz

Preserved railway / Chemin de fer préservé touristique / Museumseisenbahn

Racecourse / Hippodrome / Pferderennbahn

Skiing / Piste de ski / Skilaufen

Viewpoint / Belvédère / Aussichtspunkt

Wildlife park / Parc animalier / Wildpark

Zoo / Zoo / Tiergarten

GENERAL FEATURES

Buildings
Wood
Lighthouse (in use)
Lighthouse (disused)
Windmill
Radio or TV mast
Youth hostel
Civil aerodrome — with Customs facilities / without Customs facilities
Heliport
Public telephone
Motoring organisation telephone

WATER FEATURES

Canal
Lake
Marsh
Bridge
Ferry
Short ferry routes for vehicles
(boat) (hovercraft)
Ferry routes for vehicles (subject to change)
Cliff
Slopes
Flat rock
Transport for vehicles
Light-vessel
Low water mark
Foreshore
Dunes
High water mark

RAILWAYS

Standard gauge track
Narrow gauge track
Tunnel
Road crossing under or over
Level crossing
Station

ANTIQUITIES

ROMAN ROAD Roman antiquity
Castle · Other antiquities
Native fortress
Site of battle (with date)
------ Roman road (course of)
Ancient Monuments and Historic Buildings in the care of the Secretaries of State for the Environment, for Scotland and for Wales and that are open to the public.

RELIEF HEIGHTS IN FEET

Feet	Metres
3000	914
2000	610
1400	427
1000	305
600	183
200	61
0	0

·274 Heights in feet above mean sea level
Contours at 200ft intervals
To convert feet to metres multiply by 0·3048

BOUNDARIES

+ - + - + - + - National
- - - - - - County, Region or Islands Area

Scale
1:190 080
3 miles = 1 inch

1 kilometre = 0·6214 mile   1 mile = 1·61 kilometres

Kilometres
8 5 0 5 10 15

Miles
5 0 5 10

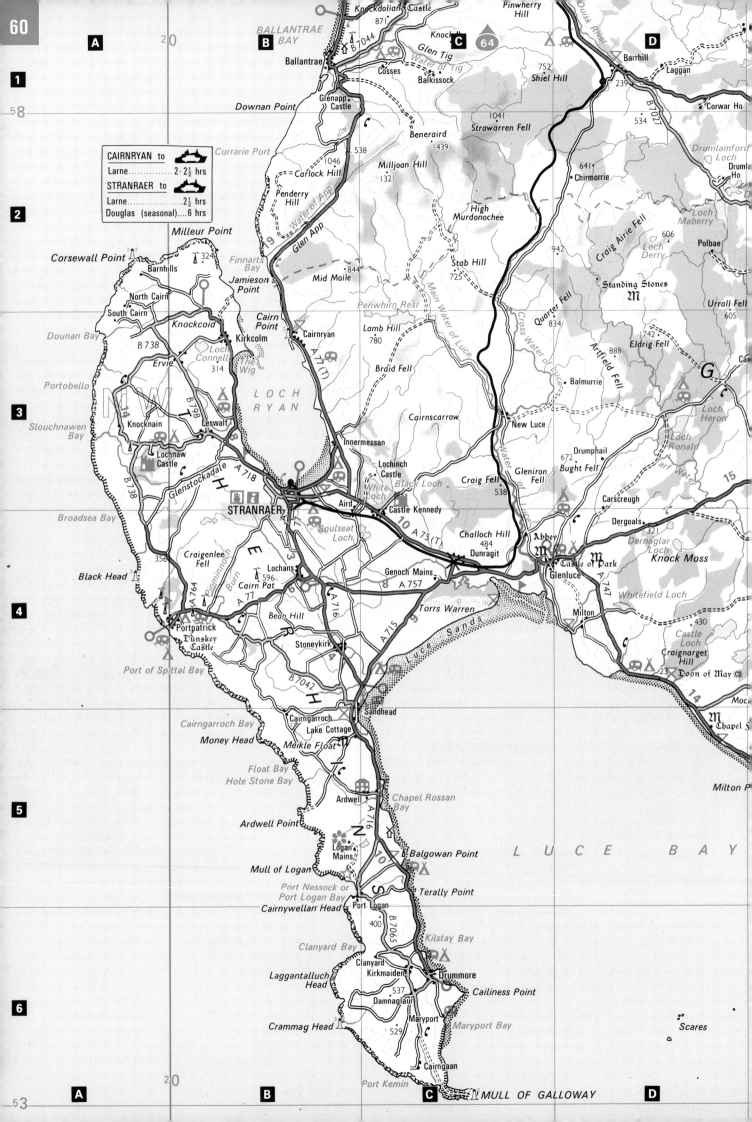

A   20   B   BALLANTRAE BAY   C   64   D

Knockdolian Castle   Pinwherry Hill   Duisk River

871   Knock H.

1   Ballantrae   B 7044   Cosses   Glen Tig   Water of Tig   Barrhill   Laggan

58   Balkissock   Shiel Hill   752   239   B 702   Corwar Ho

Downan Point   Glenapp Castle   534

Currarie Port   538   1046   Beneraird   1041   Strawarren Fell   Drumlamford Loch   Drumla Ho

Carlock Hill   1439

Milljoan Hill   641   Chirmorrie

2   Penderry Hill   1321   High Murdonochee   Loch Maberry

CAIRNRYAN to
Larne............ 2-2½ hrs
STRANRAER to
Larne................2½ hrs
Douglas (seasonal)....6 hrs

Milleur Point   Glen App   942   Craig Airie Fell   606   Loch Derry   Polbae

Corsewall Point   324   Finnarts Bay   Stab Hill   844   Mid Moile   725   Standing Stones   1742   Urrall Fell   605

Barnhills   Jamieson's Point   Penwhirn Resr   Quarter Fell   834   Eldrig Fell   888

North Cairn   Cairn Point   Cairnryan   Lamb Hill   780   Artfield Fell   G

South Cairn   Knockcoid   Kirkcolm   Braid Fell   Balmurrie   Ca

3   Dounan Bay   B 738   Loch Connell   314   The Wig   Cairnscarrow   New Luce   Loch Heron

Ervie   Portobello   B 798   LOCH RYAN   Craig Fell   Gleniron Fell   Drumphail   672   Bught Fell   Loch Ronald

Slouchnawen Bay   Knocknain   Leswalt   Innermessan   538   Carscreugh   15

Lochnaw Castle   Lochinch Castle   Abbey   Dergoals

A 718   Aird   White Loch   Black Loch   Castle of Park   321   Dernaglar Loch

Glenstockadale   STRANRAER   Castle Kennedy   Glenluce   Knock Moss

Broadsea Bay   B 738   356   Craigenlee Fell   Soulseat Loch   Challoch Hill   A 747   Whitefield Loch

Black Head   Craigenlee Fell   Lochans   Genoch Mains   484   Dunragit   Milton   430

A 764   Cairn Pat   596   A 77   A 716   8 A 757   Torrs Warren   Castle Loch

4   Portpatrick   Bean Hill   A 715   Luce Sands   Craignarget Hill

Dunskey Castle   Stoneykirk   23   Doon of May

Port of Spittal Bay   B 7042   14   Moc

Cairngarroch Bay   Sandhead   Chapel S

Cairngarroch   Lake Cottage

Money Head   Meikle Float

Float Bay   Hole Stone Bay   Ardwell   Chapel Rossan Bay

5   Ardwell Point   A 716   Balgowan Point   L U C E   B A Y

Logan Mains   Mull of Logan   Terally Point

Port Nessock or Port Logan Bay   Kilstay Bay

Cairnywellan Head   Port Logan   400   B 7065

Clanyard Bay   Laggantalluch Head   Clanyard   Kirkmaiden   Drummore   Cailiness Point

6   537   Damnaglaur   Maryport   Maryport Bay   Scares

Crammag Head   529   Cairngaan

53   Port Kemin   MULL OF GALLOWAY   Milton P

A   20   B   C   D

27
9 gford

A711
River Dee

66 B

Gelston
B736
B721

Palnackie

DALBEATTIE
C FOREST

B793

Kirkbean

Caulkerbush D
A710

E

A

1

Tongland

Screel Hill
1283
Bengairn

Tower

Kippford
or Scaur
Mote of Mark
Rockcliffe

Sandyhills
Colvend

67

Southerness

Southerness
Point

Mersehead Sands

KIRKCUDBRIGHT

55

N X

Barcloy Hill

Auchencairn

Rough
Island

Castlehill
Point

Auchencairn
Bay

Hestan Island

Kirkcarswell

A711

17

61

A711

599

Dundrennan

Abbey
534

Rascarrel

Orroland

Balcary Point

Rascarrel Bay

Dubmill P

2 almae

Townhead

Netherlaw
353

Port Mary

Wall Hill Abbey Head

Allonby B

oss

S
O
L
W
A
Y

Crosscanonby
Crosb

3

MARYPORT

A594

ROMAN

Flimby

Brou
Moor

Seaton

304

Broughto

Camerton

Bridgefor

9

Great
Clifton

A595

WORKINGTON

A66(T)

Winscales

13

C

Moss Bay

A596(T)

4

Harrington

8

Branthwaite

Distington

Ull

Lowca

Gilgarran

Pica

Moresby
565

Asby

Parton

River Keekle

Arleedon

691

WHITEHAVEN

Moresby
Parks

B5295

Frizington

Saltom Bay

CLEATOR
MOOR

B5345

5

Sandwith
462

A595(T)

Cleator

St Bees Head

Rottington

EGREMONT

459

695

St Bees

R Ehen

Haile

950

R Calder

51

Nethertown

R Ower

Beckermet

6

27

Braystones

Calder
Bridge

Works

E

Sellafield Sta

B5344

A   **B**   **C**   **D**   **E**

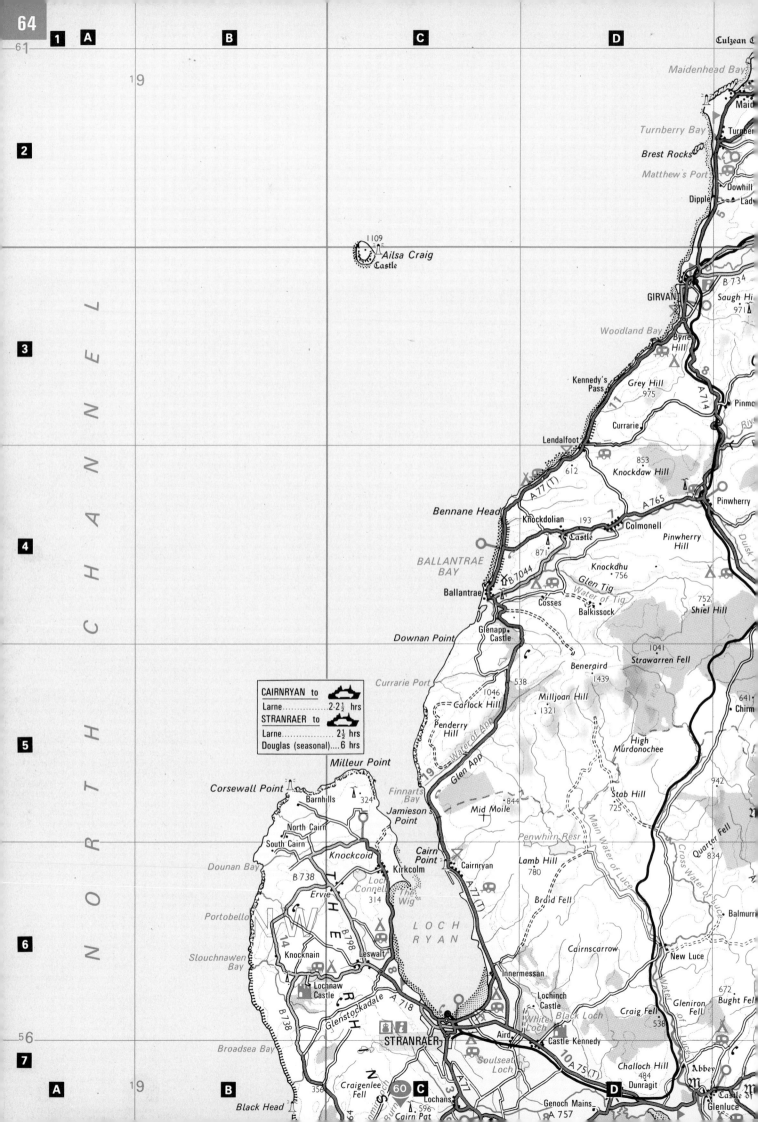

19

NORTH CHANNEL

Ailsa Craig
Castle
1109

Maidenhead Bay
Turnberry Bay
Brest Rocks
Matthew's Port
Maid
Turnbe
Dowhill
Dipple   Lady

GIRVAN
Saugh Hi
971
Woodland Bay
Byne
Hill
Kennedy's
Pass
Grey Hill
975
Currarie
Pinmo
B 734
A 714
A 77 (T)

Lendalfoot
612
853
Knockdaw Hill
A 765
Pinwherry
Bennane Head
Knockdolian
193
Colmonell
Pinwherry
Hill
Castle
871
Knockdhu
756
BALLANTRAE
BAY
B 7044
Glen Tig
Water of Tig
752
Shiel Hill
Ballantrae
Cosses
Balkissock

Downan Point
Glenapp
Castle
1041
Strawarren Fell
Benergird
1439
Currarie Port
1046
Carlock Hill
538
Milljoan Hill
1321
Penderry
Hill
641
Chirm

CAIRNRYAN to
Larne .... 2-2½ hrs
STRANRAER to
Larne .... 2½ hrs
Douglas (seasonal)....6 hrs

High
Murdonochee
942
Milleur Point
Finnarts
Bay
19
Glen App
Stab Hill
844
725
Corsewall Point
Barnhills
324
Jamieson's
Point
Mid Moile
Penwhirn Resr
North Cairn
Cairn
Point
Cairnryan
Lamb Hill
780
Quarter Fell
834
Dounan Bay
South Cairn
Knockcoid
B 738
Kirkcolm
A 77 (T)
Brid Fell
Balmurr
Loch
Connell
314
The
Wig
LOCH
RYAN
Ervie
Portobello
B 798
Cairnscarrow
New Luce
14
Knocknain
Leswalt
Innermessan
672
Gleniron
Fell
Bught Fe
Slouchnawen
Bay
8
Lochinch
Castle
Craig Fell
538
Lochnaw
Castle
Black Loch
White's
Loch
Glenstockadale
A 718
Challoch Hill
484
Dunragit
B 738
STRANRAER
Aird
Castle Kennedy
10 A 75 (T)
Broadsea Bay
Soulseat
Loch
A 757
Genoch Mains
Glenluce

19

Black Head
Craigenlee
Fell
356
Cairn Pat
596
Lochans

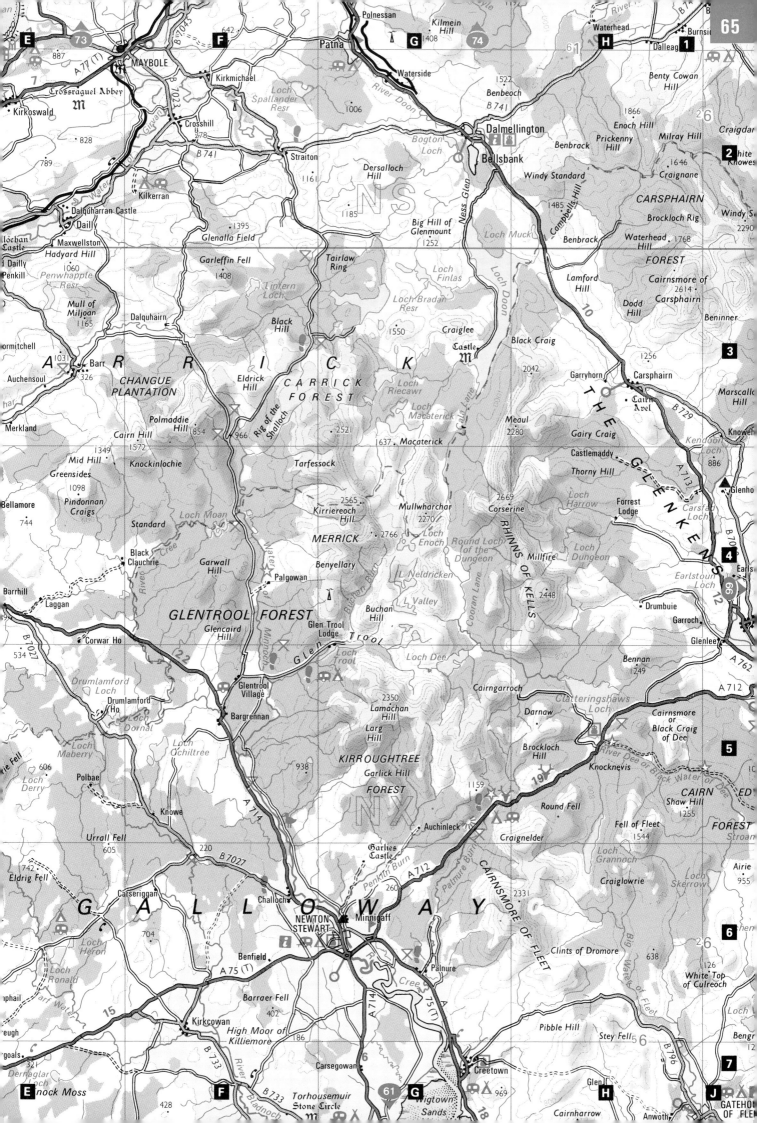

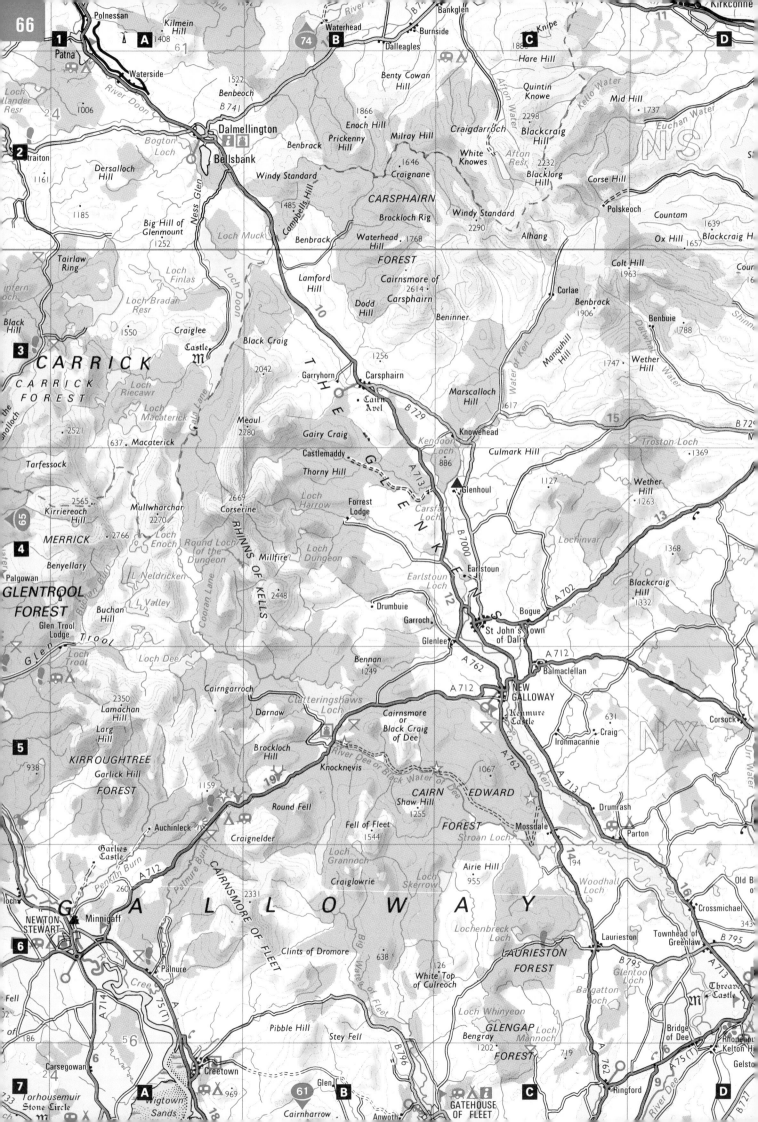

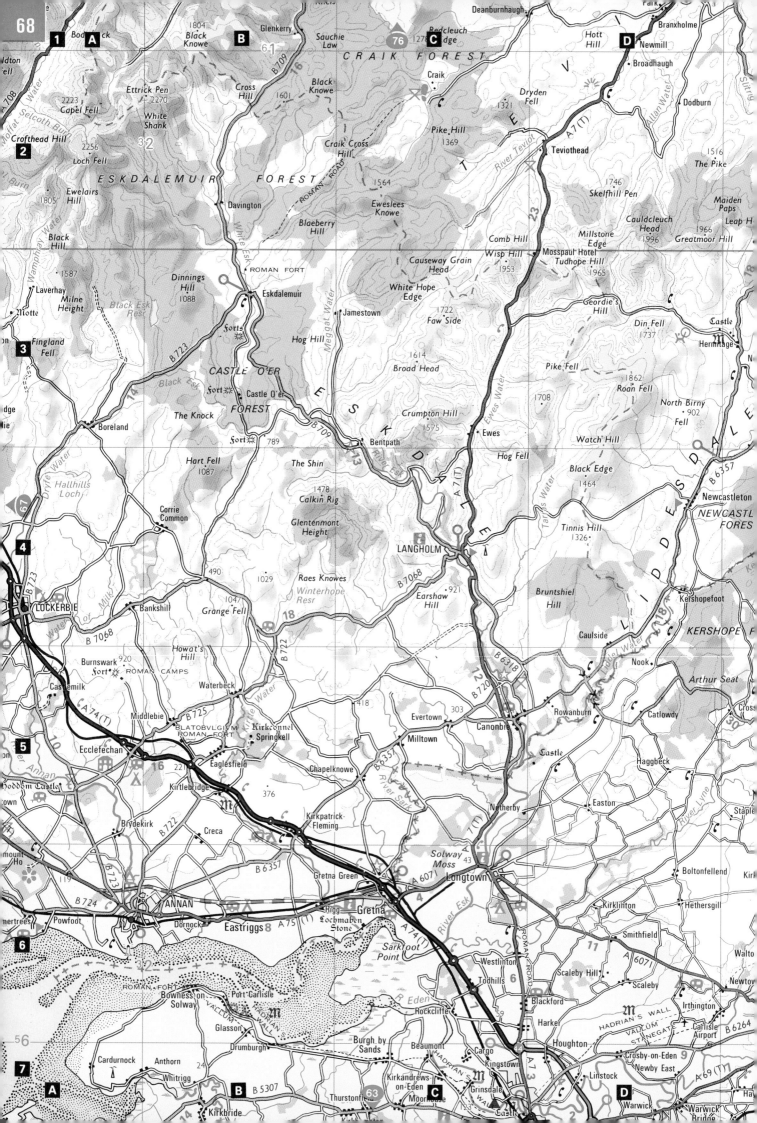

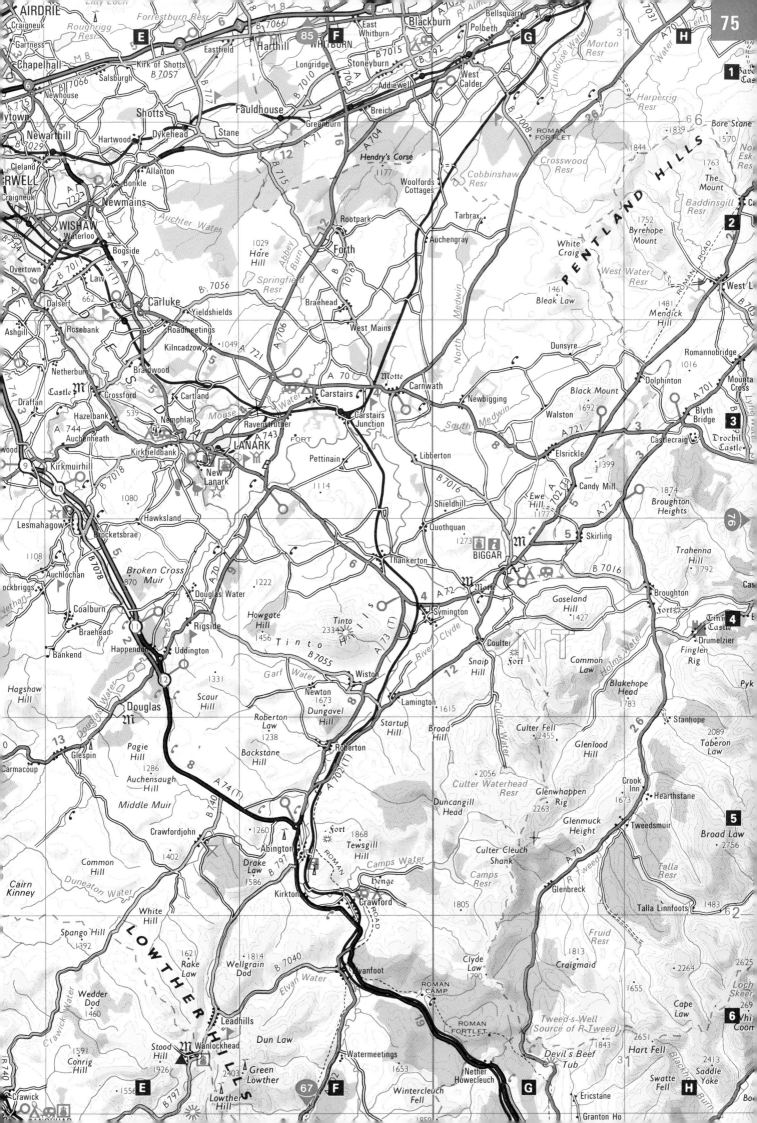

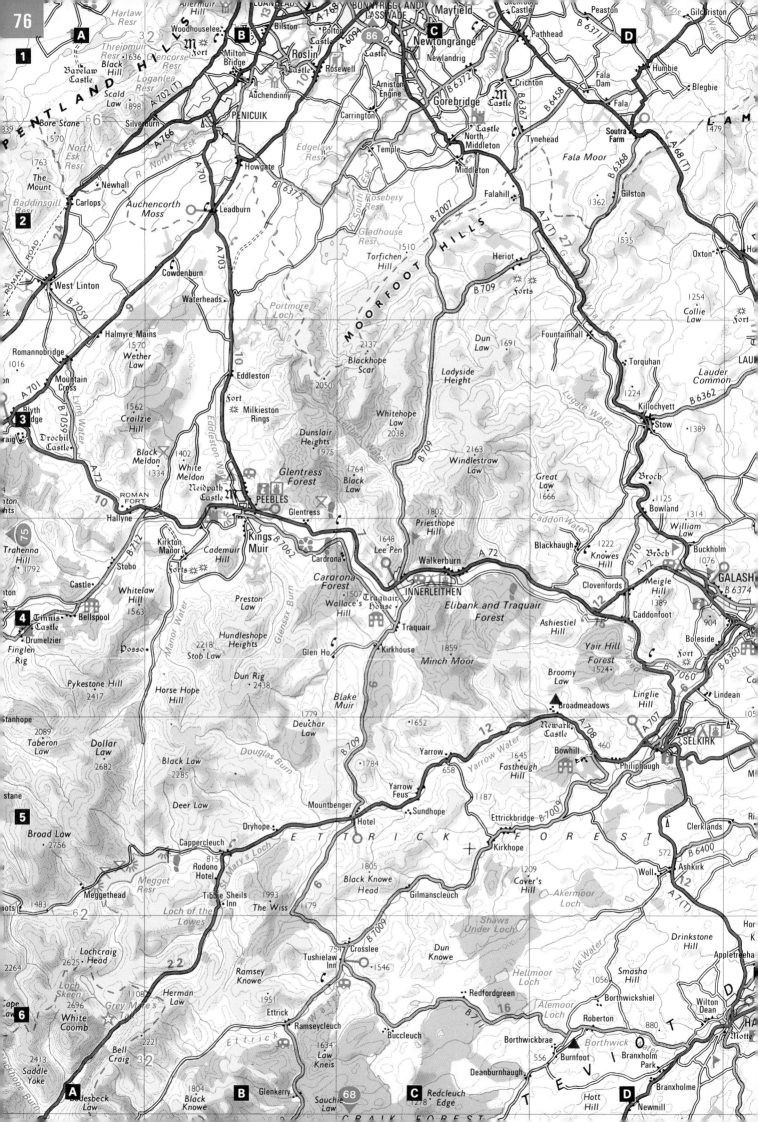

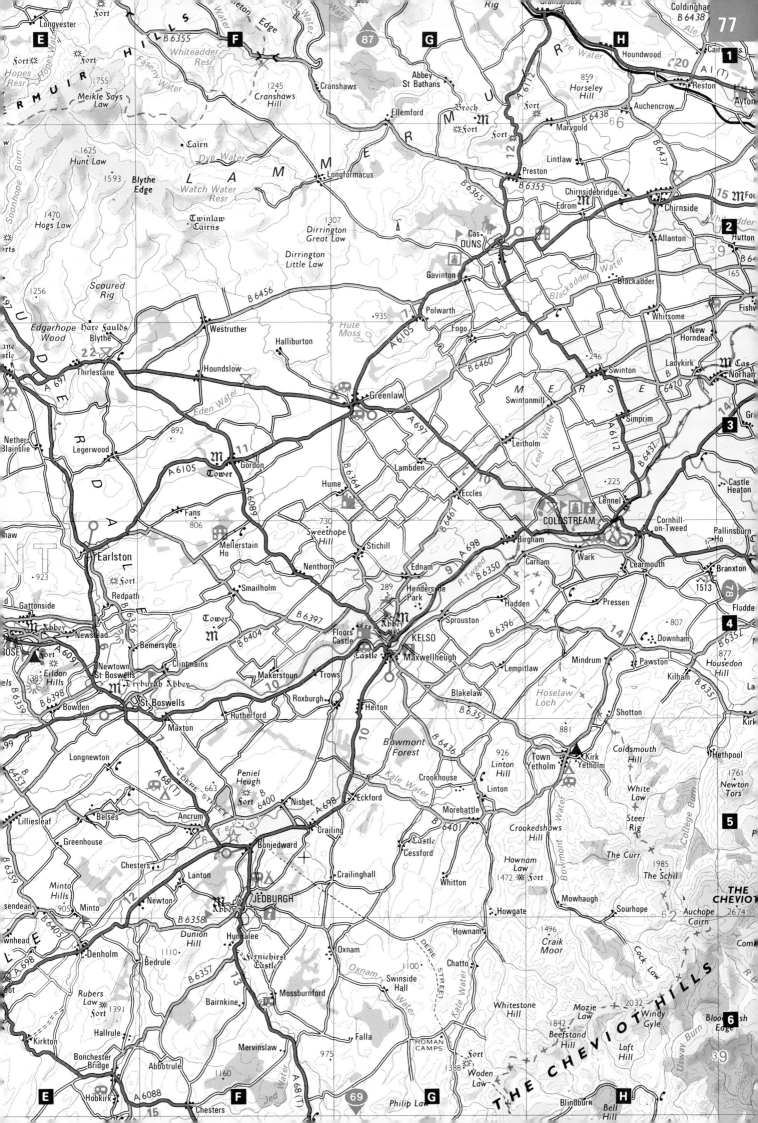

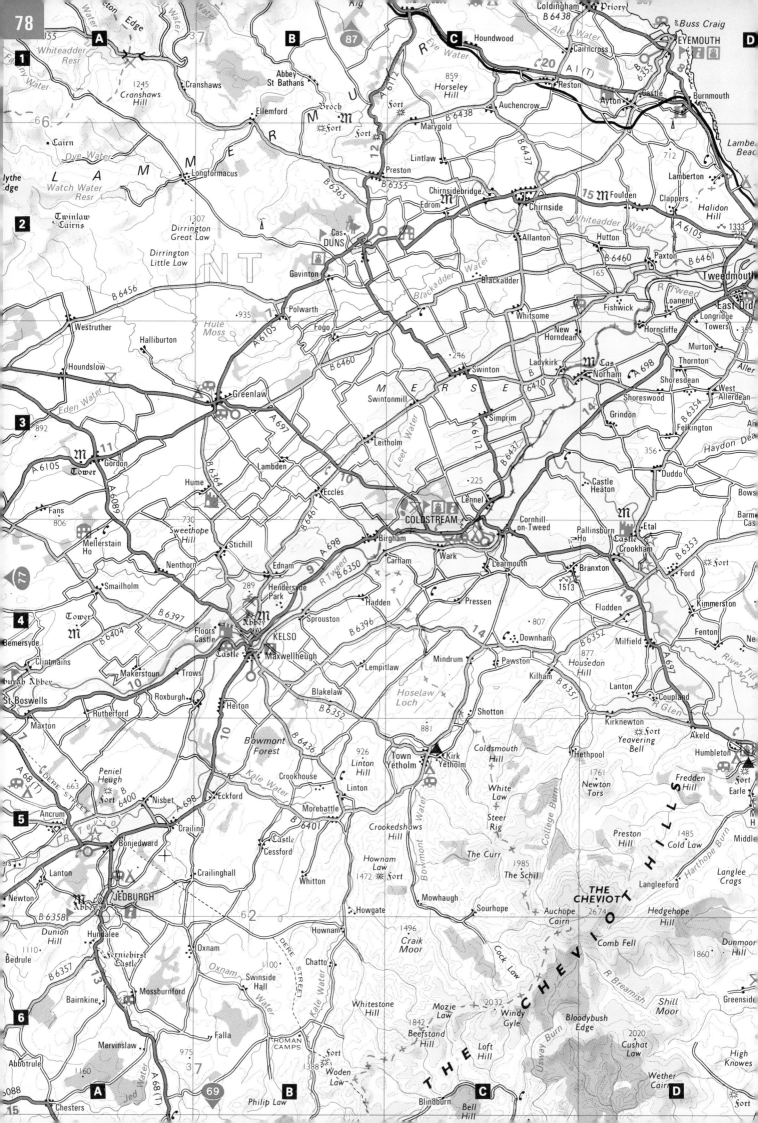

E F G 43 H

1

6 6

2

BERWICK-UPON-TWEED

Spittal

Redshin Cove

Scremerston

*Cheswick
Black Rocks*

Cheswick

Goswick

Haggerston
Castle

Berrington

Beal

269

B 6353

Lowick

Kyloe

Fenwick

*Holy Island
Sands*

Emmanuel Head

HOLY ISLAND

Holy
Island

Lindisfarne

Castle

Priory

Castle Point

Guile Point

3

*Kyloe
Hills*

Fort

Buckton

Holburn

Elwick

Ross

Detchant

Middleton

*Budle
Bay*

8 1342

Inner Sound

Castle

FARNE ISLANDS

Staple Sound

674

692

N U

Belford

Waren
Mill

Easington

Budle

Bamburgh

4

Hazelrigg

Spindlestone

Burton

B 1341

B 1340

fort

fort

Horton

Weetwood
Hall

B 6349

9

Warenton

Bellshill

Mousen

Bradford

Lucker

Elford

Seahouses

North
Sunderland

Newham
Hall

Wooler

6348

Fowberry
Tower

Greendykes

B 6348

Adderstone

Newham

Swinhoe

Beadnell

547

Chatton

Warenford

West Fleetham

*Beadnell
Bay*

Haugh
Head

Chillingham
Castle

1034

fort

394

Newstead

Chathill

High
Newton
by-the-
Sea

Snook Point

Newtown

Hepburn

Ellingham

Tower
Preston

*St Mary's
or
Newton Haven*

5

East Lilburn

Lilburn
Tower

876

*Middle
Moor*

Brunton

*Embleton
Bay*

Roseden

245

Old Bewick

fort

*Cateran
Hill*

Brownieside

North
Charlton

Christon
Bank

Embleton

*Dunstanburgh
Castle*

derton

Wooperton

17

West
Ditchburn

286

Rock

Dunstan

6 2

Roddam

New
Bewick

Harehope

Eglingham

B 6346

South
Charlton

553

356

Craster

Rennington

Howick

Brandon

Beanley

B 6346

Littlehoughton

*Howick
Haven*

Ingram

Branton

Powburn

764

Titlington

Shawdon
Hall

*Hulne
Priory*

1093

B 1340

A (T)

Longhoughton

6

Glanton
Pike

Glanton

Bolton

Abberwick

*Hulne
Park*

819

Denwick

Boulmer

1096

Great
Ryle

Whittingham

Broome
Park

Lemmington
Hall

ALNWICK

Las

144

70

*Boulmer
Haven*

Prendwick

Little
Ryle

701

B 6341

Thrunton

Hawkhill

Bilton

Lesbury

43

Alnmouth

Alnmouth

E F G H

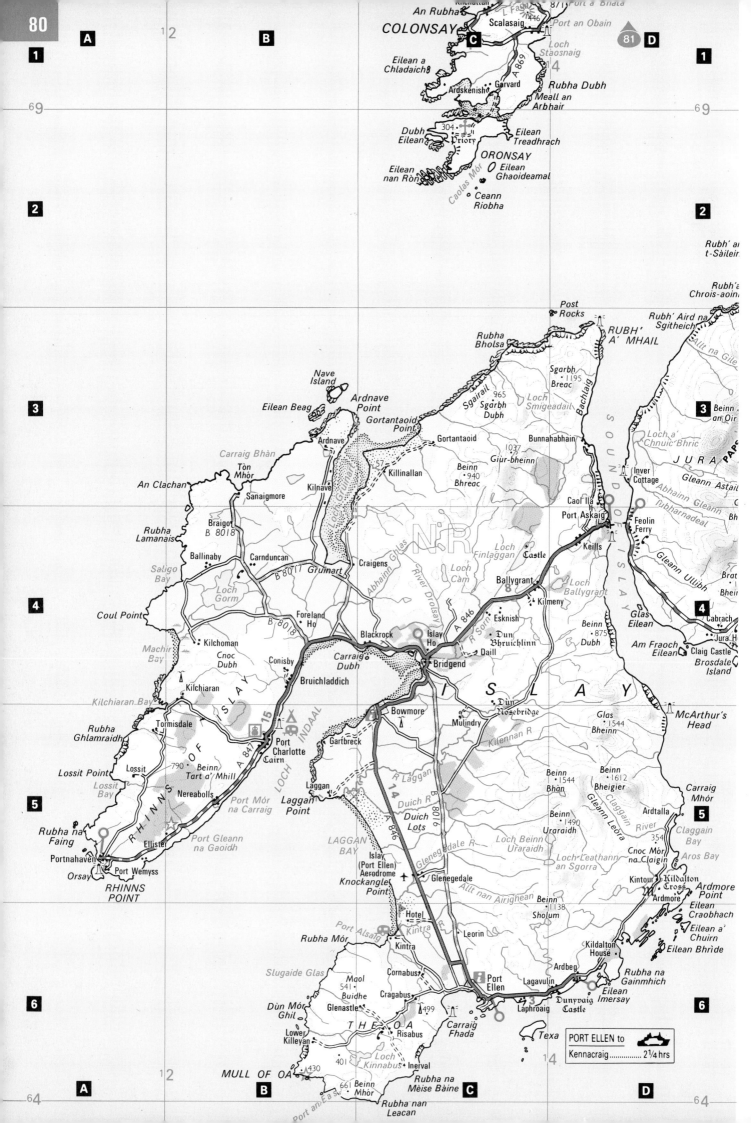

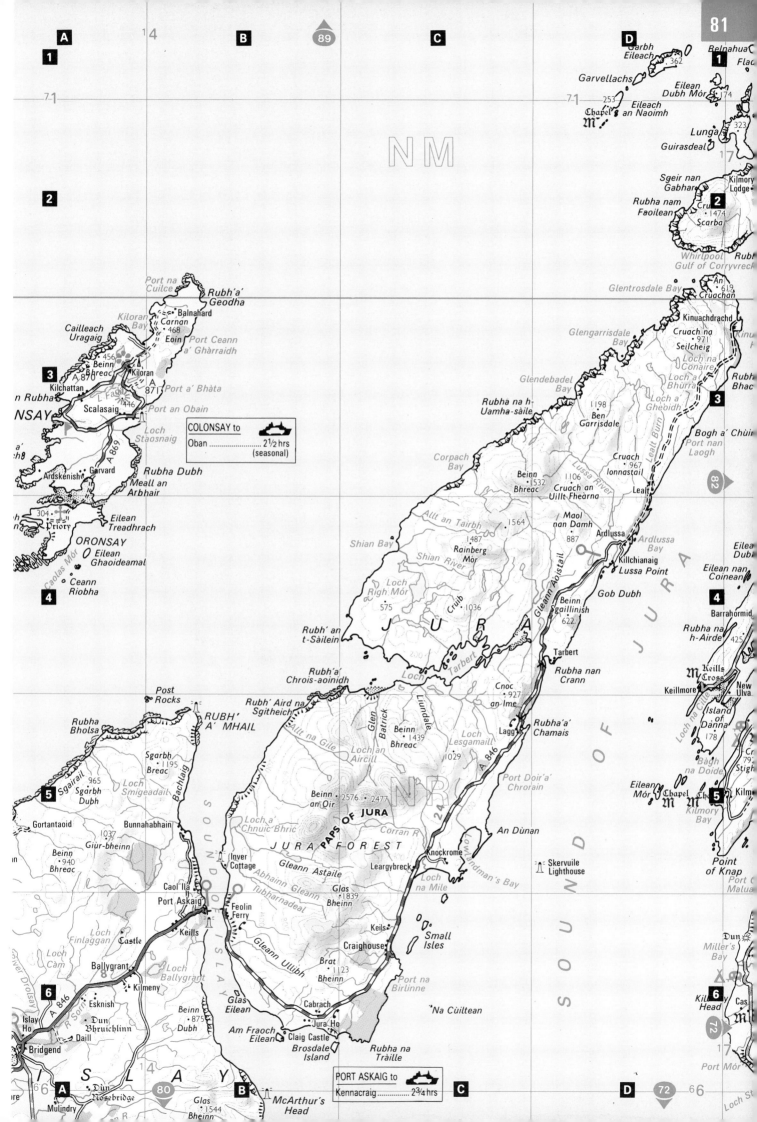

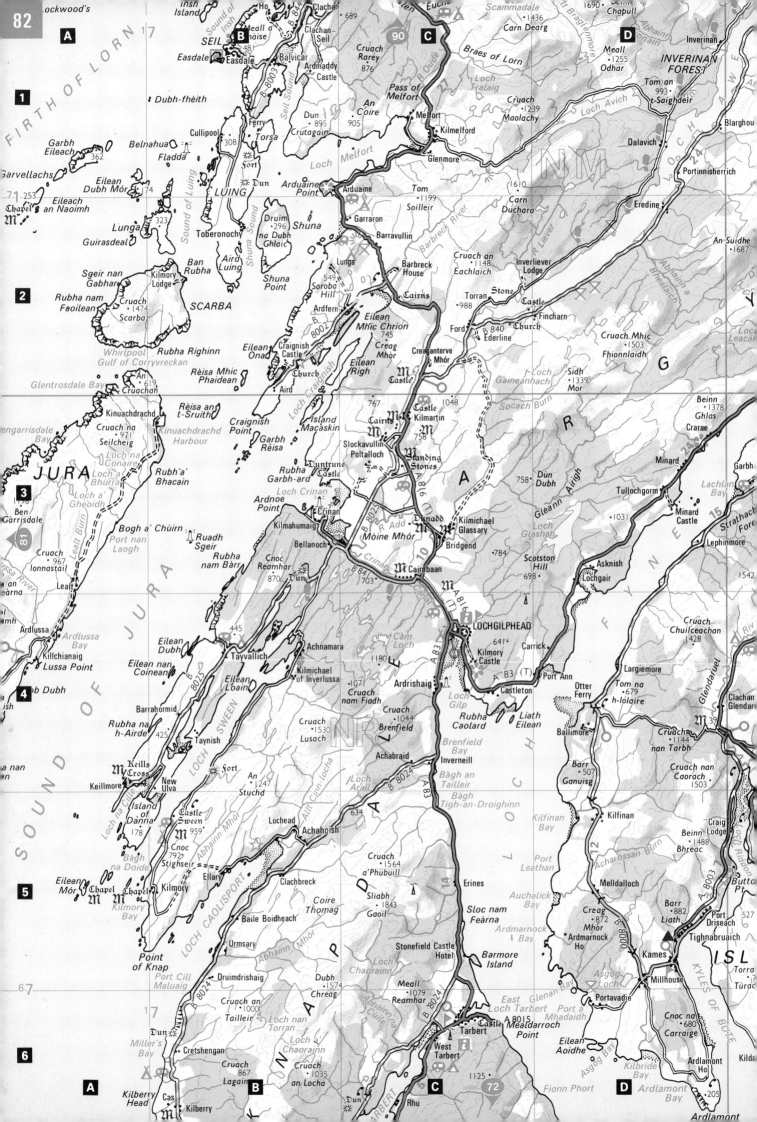

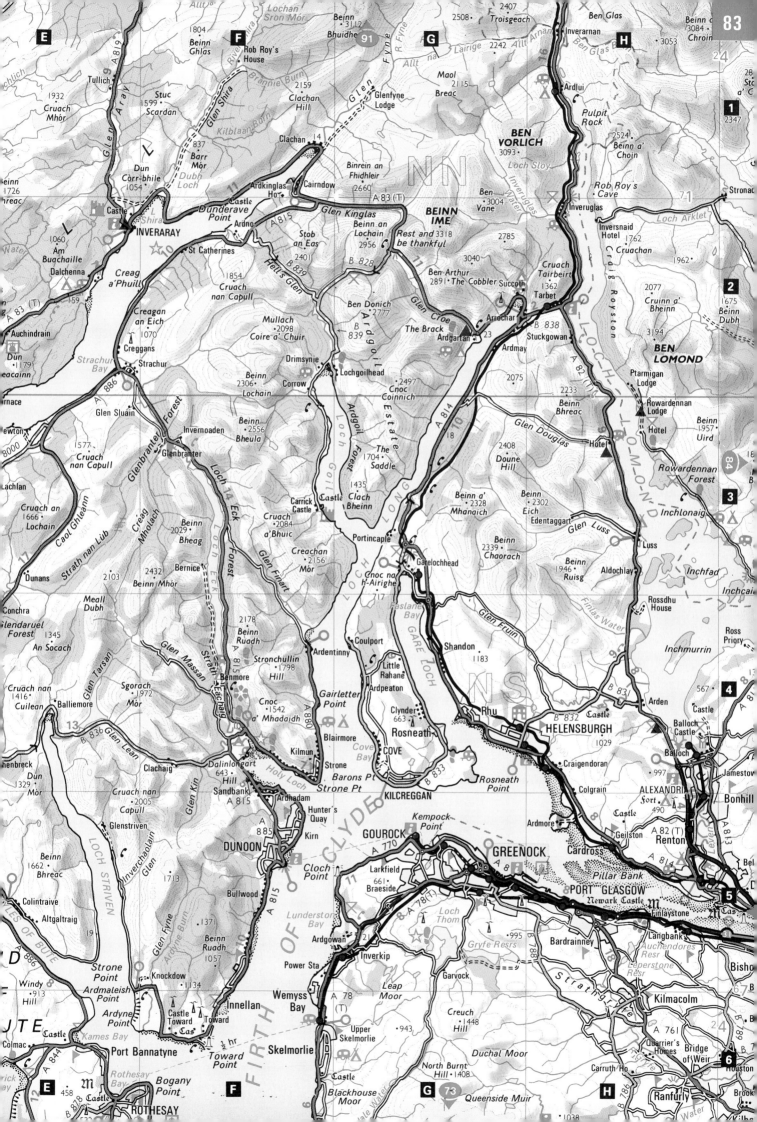

E   F   95 G   H   J

39

1

Kinkell Ness
Buddo Ness
Babbet Ness
Boarhills
10
Kingsbarns
Cambo Ness
Carr Brigs
Dunino
North Carr
Tullybothy Craigs
Balcomie
FIFE NESS
71
B 940
CRAIL
West Ness
A 917 4
KILRENNY
ANSTRUTHER
PITTENWEEM
MONANCE

2

Priory
Isle of May

3

NORTH BERWICK
Craigleith
Castle   Bass Rock
Tantallon Castle
St Baldred's Boat
613
N Berwick Law
Auldhame
Scoughall
A 198
Kingston
Whitekirk
St Baldred's Cradle
Peffer Burn
Tyne Mouth
B 1377
Tyninghame
Castle
DUNBAR
Hill
Preston
West Barns
Broxburn
Barns Ness
EAST LINTON
A 1(T)
Biel Water
B 6370
Skateraw
Power Station
Hailes Castle
Traprain
Pitcox
Spott
13
Thorntonloch
Traprain Law
Luggate Burn
737 Brunt Hill
Dry Burn
Castle
Stenton
Innerwick
GTON
Papple
Halls
Reed Point
Whitelaw Hill
Garvald
1046
Cocklaw Hill
Cockburnspath
Siccar Point
Wheat Stack
B 6370
1301
Oldhamstocks
Fast Castle
67
B 6369
636
Fort Dunbar Common
1307
Bransly Hill
Ecclaw
Fort
803
Lumsdaine
Telegraph Hill
744
Cross Law
6
Gifford
Carfrae
LAMMERMUIR HILLS
Heart Law
1283
909
Fort
Meikle Black Law
Coldingham Moor
Northfield
ester Ho
Danskine
Spartleton Edge
Blackburn Rig
Grantshouse
Coldingham
12
ester Castle
Longyester
Fort
Whiteadder Water
Monynut Edge
77
Bothwell Water
Eye Water
Houndwood
Priory
B 6438
E   F   G   H   J

4

5

39

6

NT

B 6355

Ale Water

77

09

96

1

INNER HEBRIDES

Eag na Maoile

Rubha Mór

Rubh a'
Bhinnein
Bousd
B 8072

Cliad Bay
Gallanach
Arnabost
Grishipoll
Rubha Hogh
Ballyhaugh
Ben · 340
Hogh
Loch
Cliad
B 8071
·239

Hogh Bay
Totronald
Coll Aerodrome
Arinagour
B 8070
Bagh Feis
COLL

2
Rubha a'
Ghraineig
Feall Bay
Acha
Port Mine
Arileod
B 8070
Eilean
Ornsay
Breachacha
Castle
Castle
Friesland
Calgary Point
Crossapol
Bay
Rubha Fàsachd
Port na
h-Eathar
Gunna
Port a'
Mhurain
Soa

Ihr

Urvaig

Vaul
Bay
Rubha
Port Bhiosd
Balephetrish
Bay
Vaul
Salum
Rubha Dubh
Hough
Skerries
Clachan Mór
Caolas
B 8069
Rubha Hogh
Bay
Balevullin
Ruaig
Rubha
Chràiginis
389
Kenovay
Gott Bay
Rubha
Nead a' Gheòidh

3
Kilkenneth
B 8068
Soa
B 8068
B 8065
Moss
Scarinish
Middleton
Heylipol
Heanish
TIREE

TIREE to	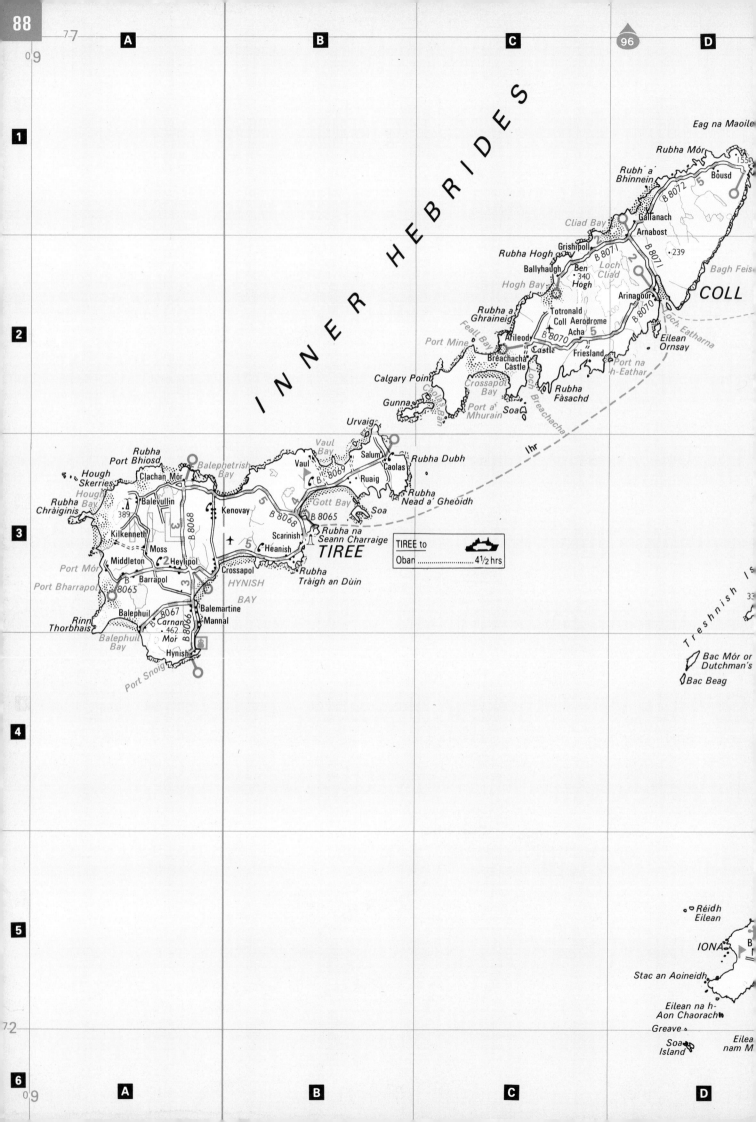
Oban .... 4½ hrs	

Port Mór
Crossapol
Rubha na
Seann Charraige
Port Bharrapol
Barrapol
HYNISH
Rubha
Tràigh an Dùin
B 8065
BAY
Balephuil
B 8067
Balemartine
Rinn
Thorbhais
Carnan
462
Mór
B 8066
Mannal
Balephuil
Bay
Hynish
Port Snoig

Treshnish Is

Bac Mór or
Dutchman's

Bac Beag

4

5

Réidh
Eilean
IONA

Stac an Aoineidh

Eilean na h-
Aon Chaorach

Greave

72

Soa
Island

Eilea
nam M

09

6

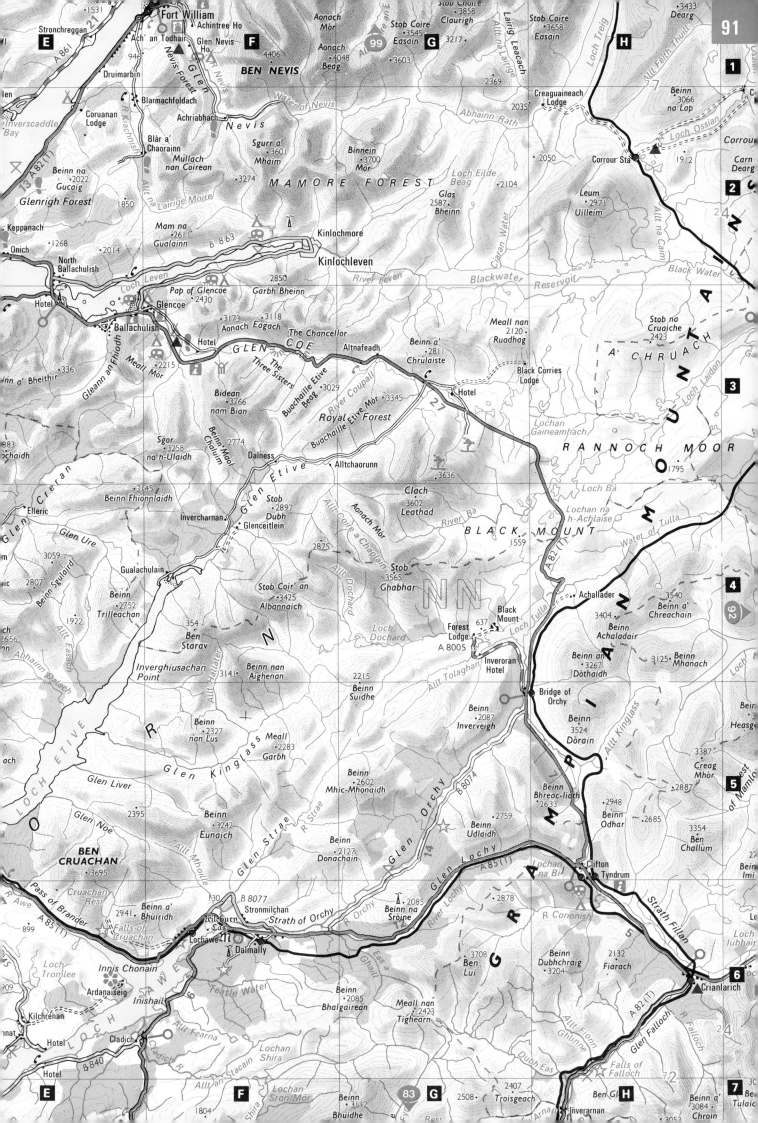

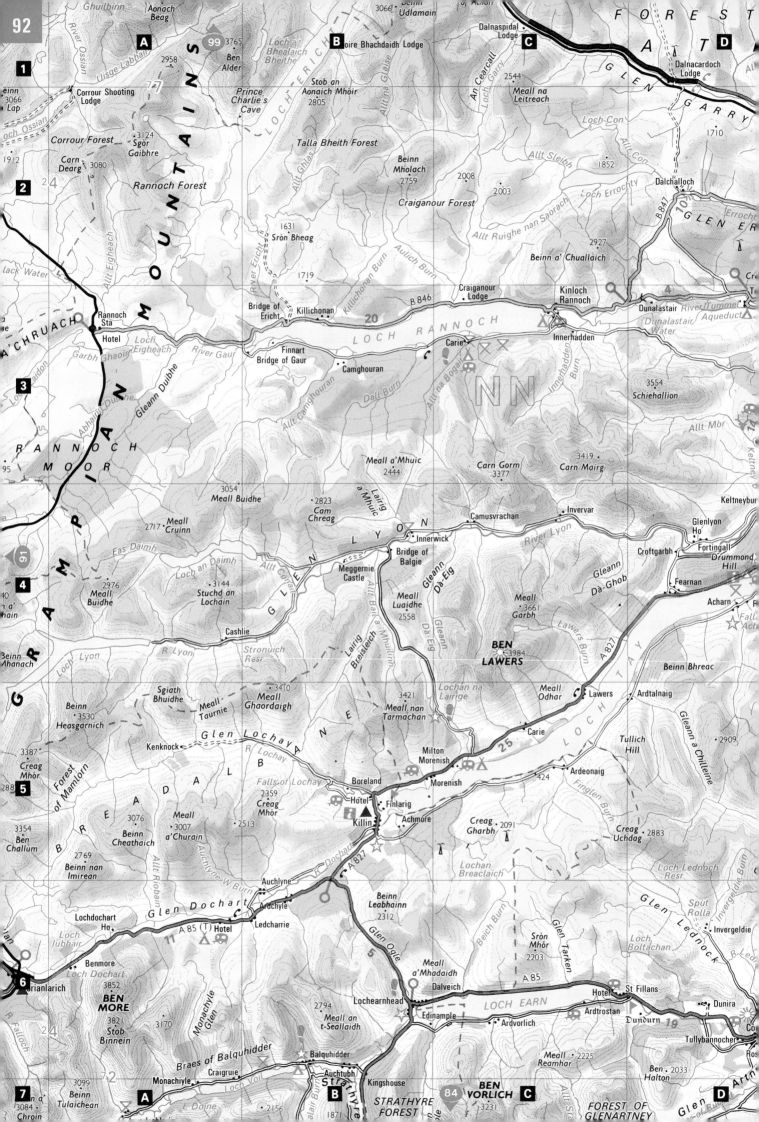

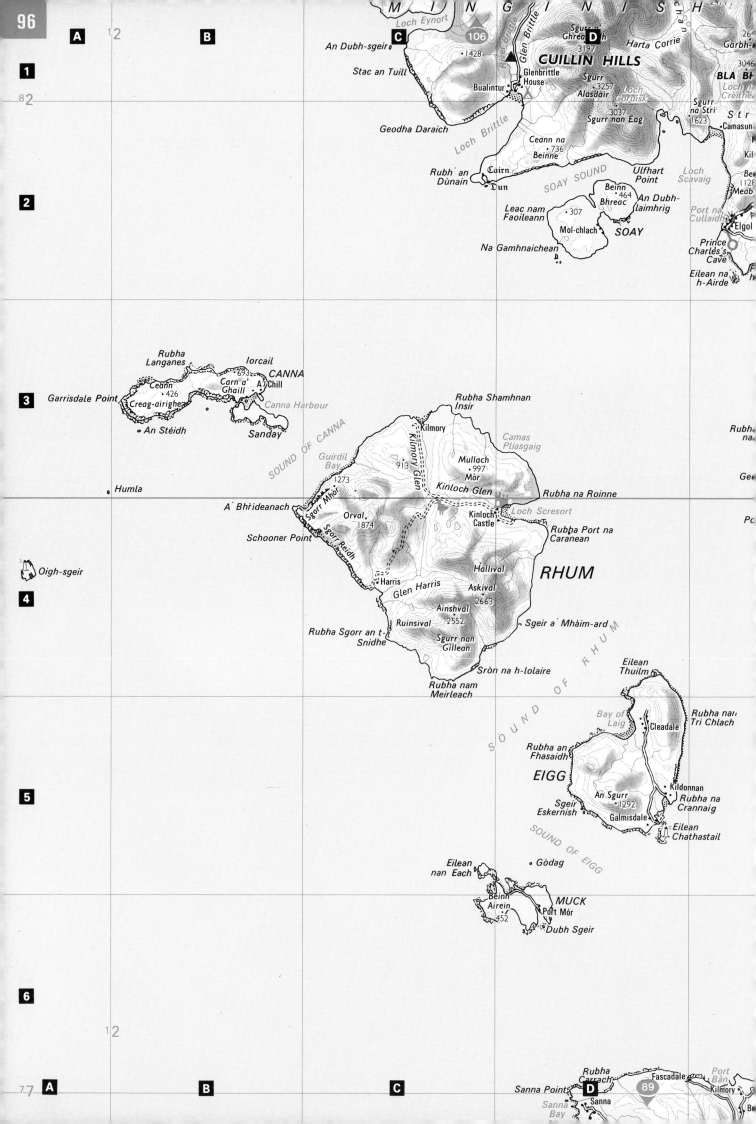

A 12 **B** **C** **D**

1

82

M I N G I N I S H
Loch Eynort
An Dubh-sgeir
Stac an Tuill
Bualintur
Geodha Daraich
106
River Brittle
Glen Brittle
Glenbrittle House
·1428
Sgurr a' Ghreadaidh
3197
CUILLIN HILLS
Harta Corrie
3046
BLA BH
Sgurr Alasdair
3257
Loch Coruisk
3037
Sgurr nan Eag
Loch Crèithe
Sgurr na Stri
·1623
Str
Camasun
Kil
Ceann na Beinne
·736
Loch Scavaig
·Ben
·1128
Meab

2

Rubh an Dùnain
Cairn
Dun
SOAY SOUND
Leac nam Faoileann
Mol-chlach
Na Gamhnaichean
Beinn Bhreac
·464
An Dubh-laimhrig
·307
SOAY
Ulfhart Point
SOAY SOUND
Port na Cullaidh
Elgol
Prince Charles's Cave
Eilean na h-Airde

3

Rubha Langanes
Iorcail
CANNA
A' Chill
Ceann
·426
Carn a' Ghaill
·693
Garrisdale Point
Creag-airighe
An Stéidh
Sanday
Canna Harbour
SOUND OF CANNA
Guirdil Bay
·913
Kilmory
Mullach Mór
·997
Camas Pliasgaig
Rubha Shamhnan Insir
Rubh
na
Gee

Humla
·1273
A' Bhrìdeanach
Sgorr Mhòr
Orval
·1874
Kinloch Glen
Kinloch Castle
Loch Scresort
Rubha na Roinne
Po

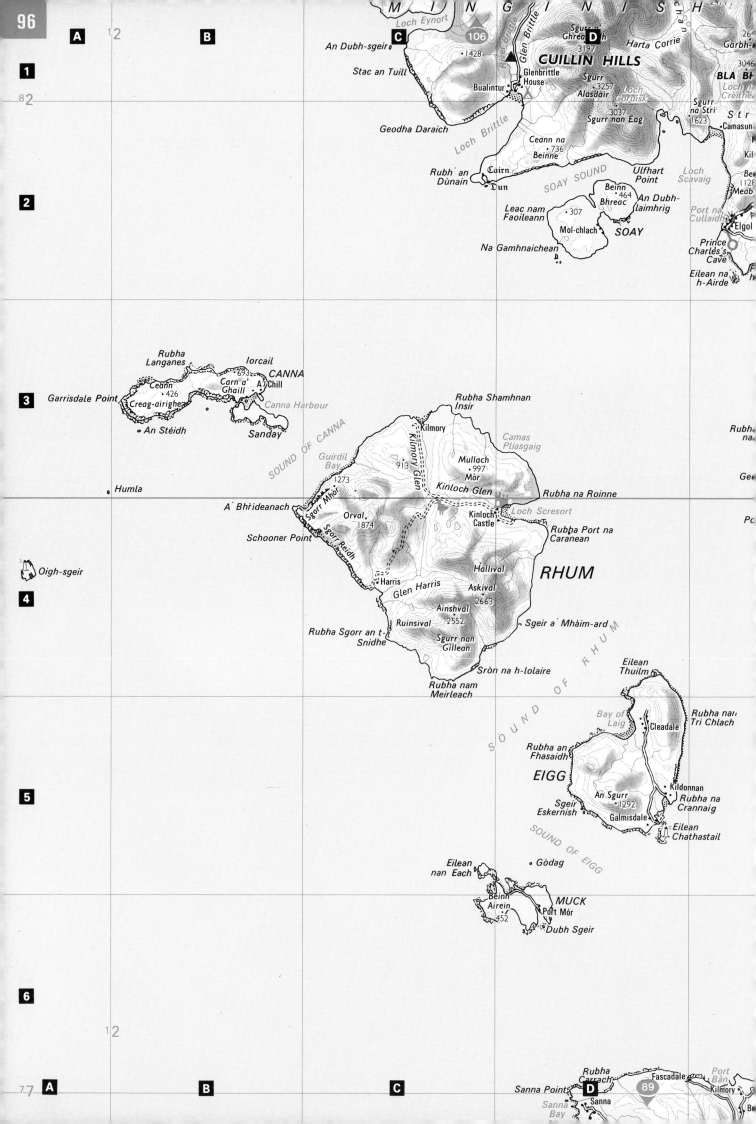 Oigh-sgeir

4

Schooner Point
Sgorr Reidh
Harris
Glen Harris
Rubha Sgorr an t-Snidhe
Ruinsival
Hallival
Askival
·2663
Ainshval
·2552
Sgurr nan Gillean
Sgeir a' Mhàim-ard
RHUM
Rubha Port na Caranean
SOUND OF RHUM

Sròn na h-Iolaire
Rubha nam Meirleach

Eilean Thuilm
Bay of Laig
Cleadale
Rubha nan Tri Chlach

5

Rubha an Fhasaidh
EIGG
Sgeir Eskernish
An Sgurr
·1292
Galmisdale
Kildonnan
Rubha na Crannaig
Eilean Chathastail
SOUND OF EIGG

Eilean nan Each
Gòdag
Beinn Airein
·452
MUCK
Port Mór
Dubh Sgeir

6

12

A **B** **C** **D**
Rubha Carrach
Sanna Point
Sanna
Sanna Bay
89
Fascadale
Port Bàn
Kilmory

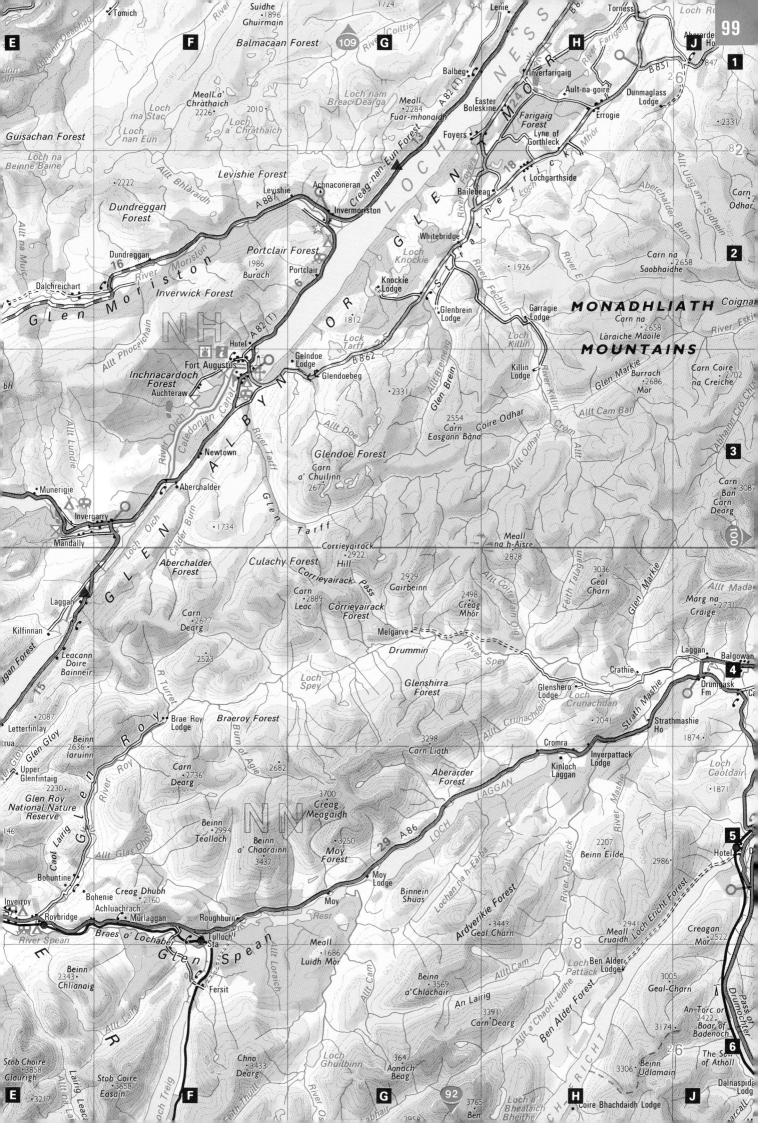

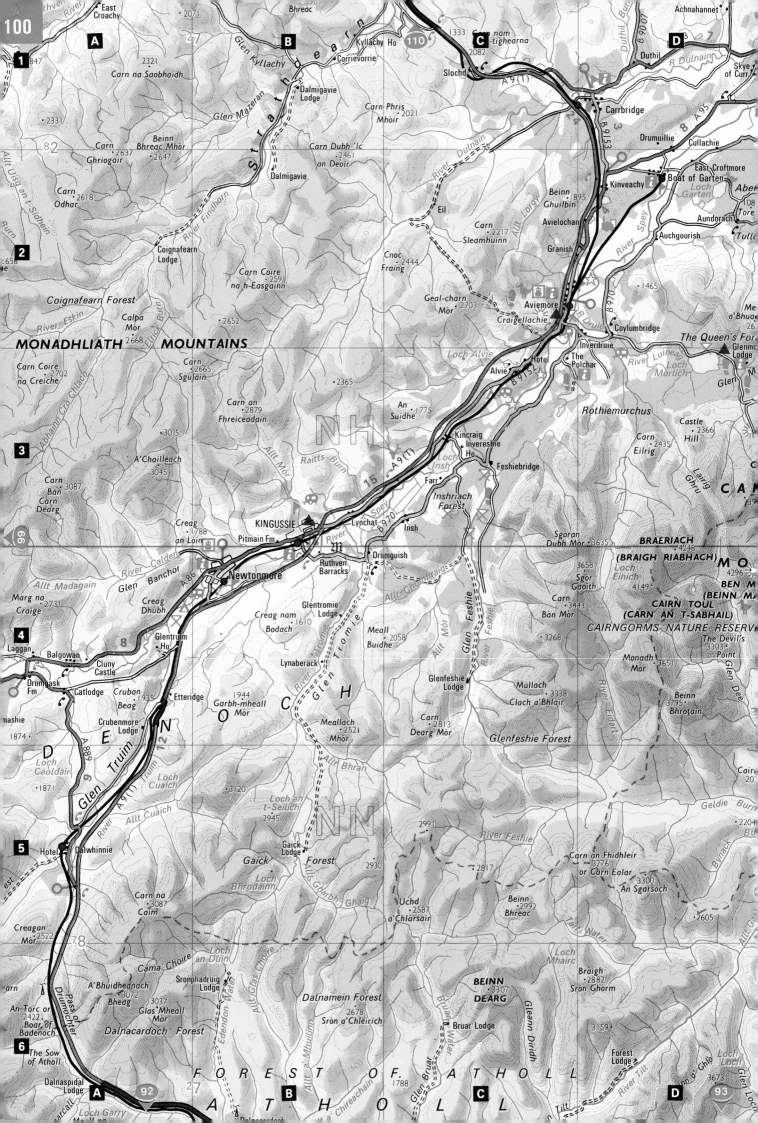

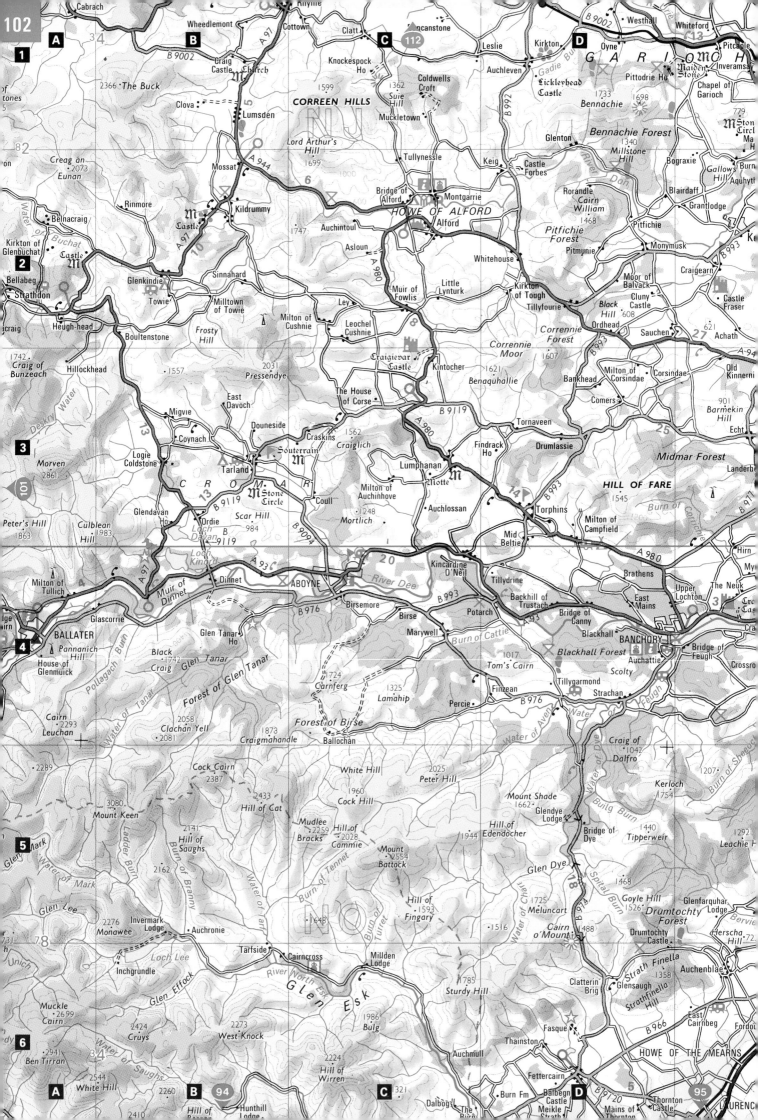

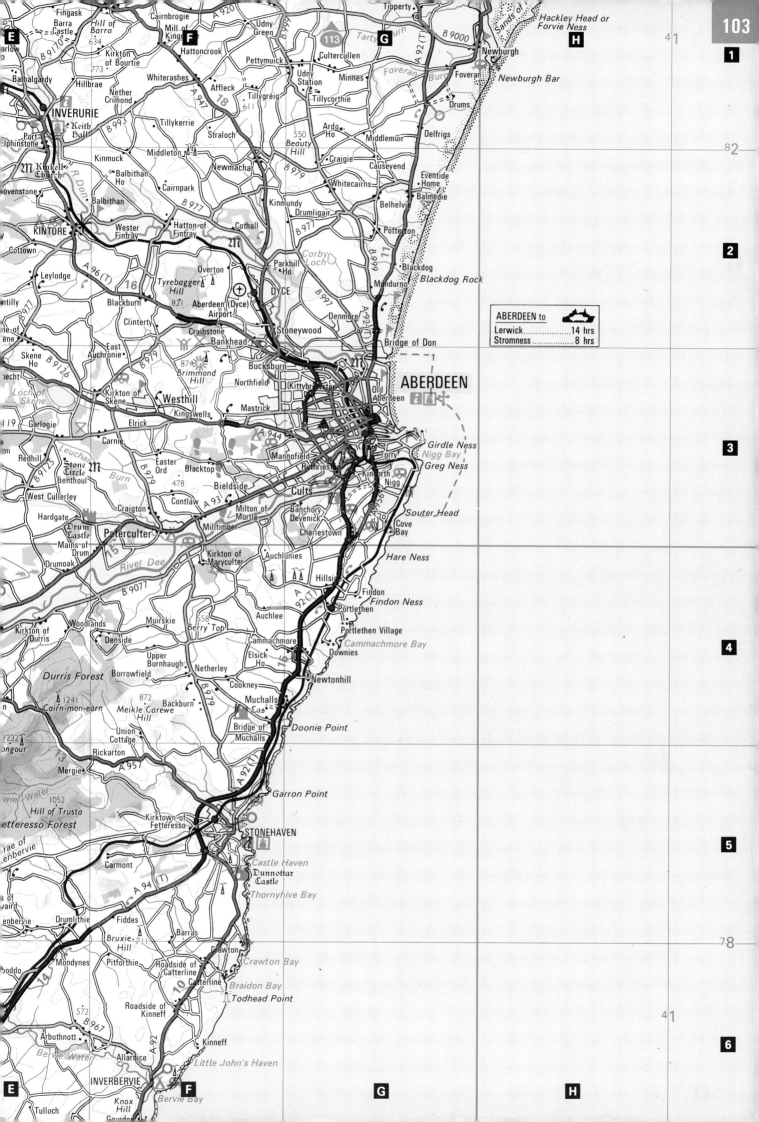

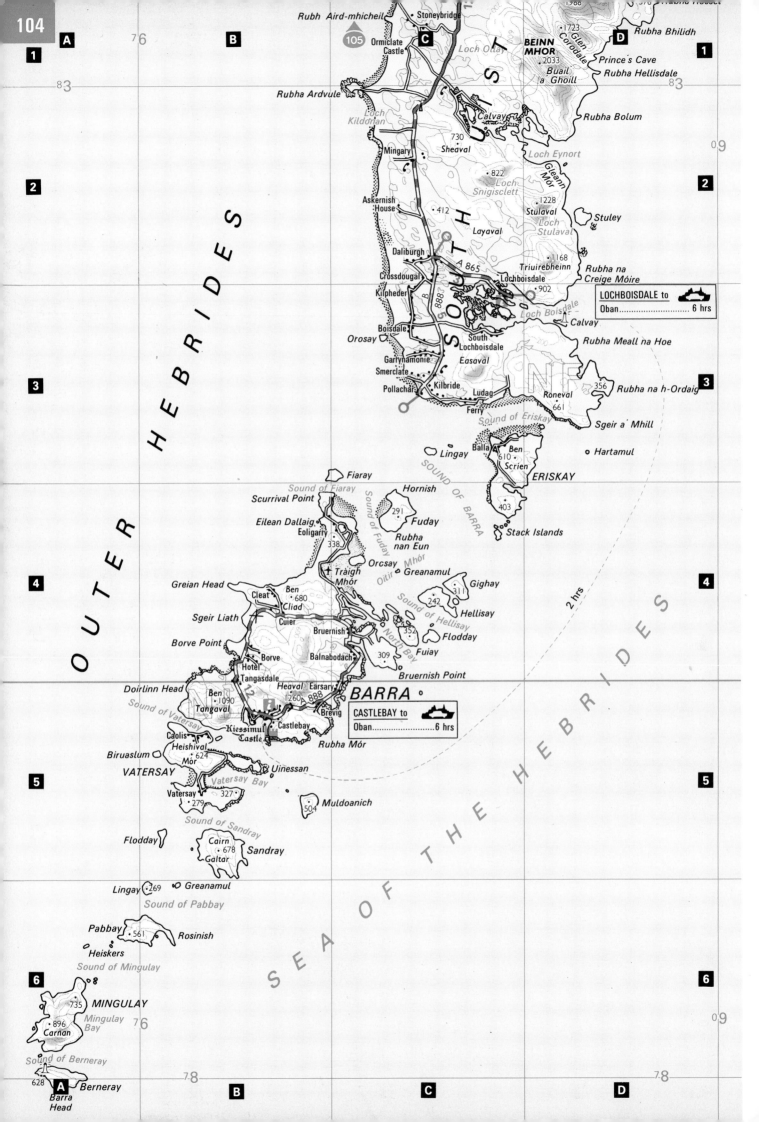

A 76 B C 105 D

1

83 83

Rubh Aird-mhicheil Stoneybridge
Ormiclate Castle Rubha Bhilidh

BEINN MHOR Glen Corodale
Rubha Hellisdale Prince's Cave
Buail a Ghoill 2033
1723

Rubha Ardvule

Loch Kildonan Calvay

Mingary Sheaval 730 Rubha Bolum

Loch Eynort 09

2

Loch Ollay

Gleann Mhor 822 Loch Snigisclett
Askernish House 412 1228 Stulaval Stuley
Layaval Loch Stulaval

Daliburgh Triuirebheinn 1168 Rubha na Creige Móire
A 865 Lochboisdale 902

Crossdougal B 888

Kilpheder

LOCHBOISDALE to
Oban .... 6 hrs

Boisdale Calvay

Orosay South Lochboisdale Rubha Meall na Hoe

3

Garrynamonie Easaval

Smerclate Rubha na h-Ordaig
Pollachar Kilbride Ludag Roneval 356
661

Ferry Sgeir a' Mhill
Sound of Eriskay

Lingay Balla Hartamul
Ben Screen 610

ERISKAY Sound of Barra

Fiaray
Sound of Fiaray Hornish 403
Scurrival Point Fuday Stack Islands
Eilean Dallaig 291
Eoligarry Rubha nan Eun
338 Orcsay Greanamul
Oitir Mhór

4

Traigh Mhór Gighay
Greian Head 311
Cleat Ben 680 Sound of Hellisay 242 Hellisay
Cliad 352
Sgeir Liath Cuier Flodday
Bruernish Fuiay
Borve Point Balnabodach 309 North Bay
Borve
Hotel Bruernish Point
Tangasdale
Doirlinn Head Heaval Earsary
Ben 1090 1260 888 **BARRA**
Tangaval 12 Brevig **CASTLEBAY to**
Kiessimul Castlebay Oban .... 6 hrs
Castle Rubha Mór

5

Caolis
Heishival Uinessan
Biruaslum Mór 624 2 hrs
VATERSAY
Vatersay 327
279 Muldoanich
Sound of Sandray 504

Flodday Cairn 678
Galtar Sandray

Lingay 269 Greanamul
Sound of Pabbay

Pabbay 561 Rosinish
Heiskers
Sound of Mingulay

6

MINGULAY 735
896 Mingulay Bay 76
Carnan

Sound of Berneray
628 Berneray 78
A B C D
Barra Head

OUTER HEBRIDES (left side, vertical)

SEA OF THE HEBRIDES (right side, vertical)

OUTER HEBRIDES

NORTH UIST

BENBECULA

SOUTH UIST

BERNERAY

EAVAL

HECLA
1988

BEINN MHOR
2033

SOUND OF MONACH

Heisker
or
Monach Islands

Haskeir Island
Haskeir Eagach

Quinish
Spuir
Sound of Spuir
Sound of Pabbay

Bein Shleibh
Ruisgarry
Borve
Baile
Ferry
Vaitam
Mas

Boreray
Rubha Bhoisnis
Aird Thormaic

Aird a'
Mhòrain
Veilish
Point
Lingay
Oronsay
Newton
Newtonferry
Torogay
Sound of Berneray
Beinn Mhor
624
Crogary Mór
588
Grenitote
Sollas
Trumisgarry
Loch nan Geireann
Lochmaddy
Hotel

Sgeir Orival
Vallay
Griminish Point
Scolpaig
Balmartin
Valley Strand
A 865
Clettraval
435
Glen Drolla
Marrival
756
Loch Scadavay
332
824
North Lee
920
South Lee

Manish Point
Rubha Dubh Tighary
Tigharry
Hougharry
Causamul
Aird an Rùnair
Balranald
Rubha Port Scolpaig
Bayhead
Paible
Deasker
Rubha Raouill
Oitir Fhiadhaich
Kirkibost Island

Huskeiran
Shillay
Hearnish
Stockay
Ceann Ear

Loch Huna
458
Claddach Kirkibost
Loch Langass
296
A 867
Loch Scadavay
Loch Fada
Loch Skealtar
Loch Maddy

Vorogay
Samala
Teanamachar
Baleshare
Clachan-a-Luib
Bail Uachdraich
Carinish
Loch Eport
Sidinish
Locheport
Loch Caravat
224
Loch Obisary
1139
Eigneig
Eigneig B
Rubha Gille-m

Eachkamish
Oitir Mhór
Liernish
Floddaybeg
Floddaymore
Ronay
379
Rubha na Rodagrich
325
Maragay Mór

Beul an
Benbecula Aerodrome
Uachdar
Balaglas
Grimsay
Gramsdale
Flodda
Rossinish

Balivanich
Nunton
Griminish
Rueval
408
Maaey Riabhach
Greanamul Deas

Torlum
Liniclate
Loch Heouravay
73
Loch Uiskevagh
Rubha Cam nan Gall

Hornish Point
Ardivachar Point
Ardivachar
Eochar
Creagorry
Loch a Laip
334
Wiay

Loch Bee
A 865
West Gerinish
Lochcarnan
Sandwick
Steisay
Gasay
Caltinish
Glas-eileanan
Luirsay Dubh

285
Stilligarry
B 890
Lochskipport
551
Loch Skipport
Ornish Island

Howmore
Loch Druidibeg
208
Acairseid Falaich
Mol a Tuath

Verran Island
Snishival
Usinish
576
Rubha Rossel

Rubh' Aird-mhicheil
Stoneybridge
Ormiclate Castle
Loch Ollay
Loch Olay
1723
Glen Corodale
Usinish
Rubha Bhilidh
Prince s Cave
Rubha Hellisdale

114

104

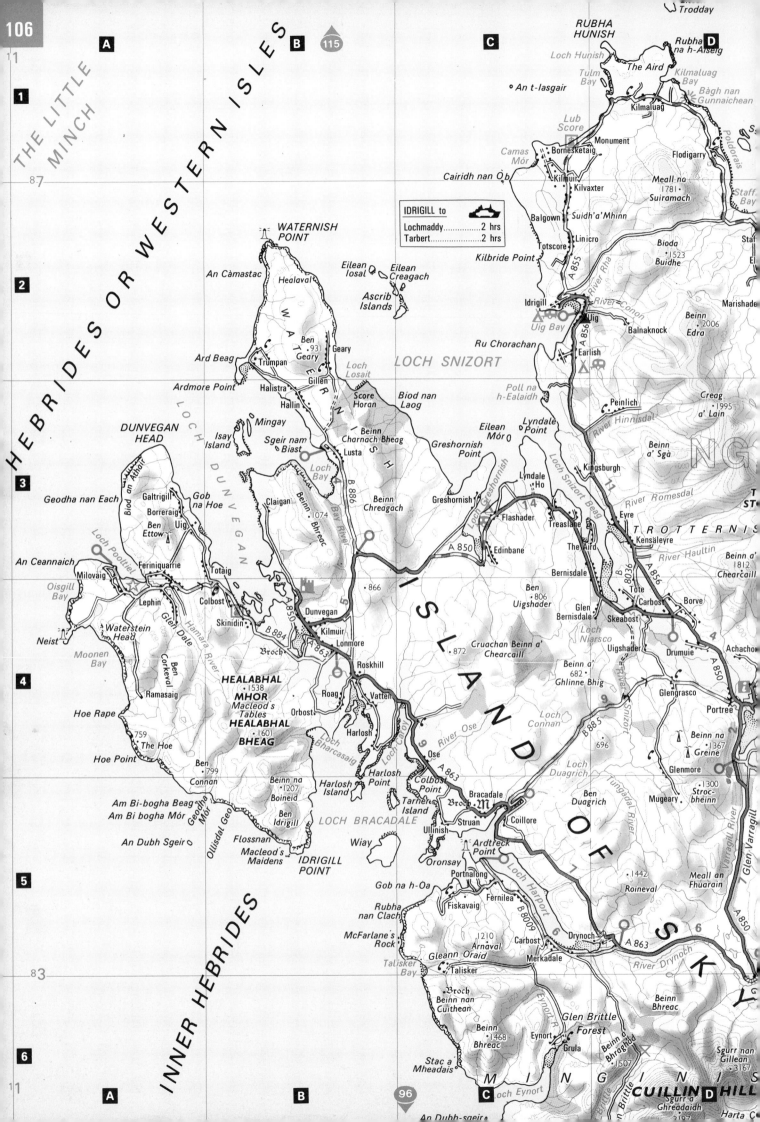

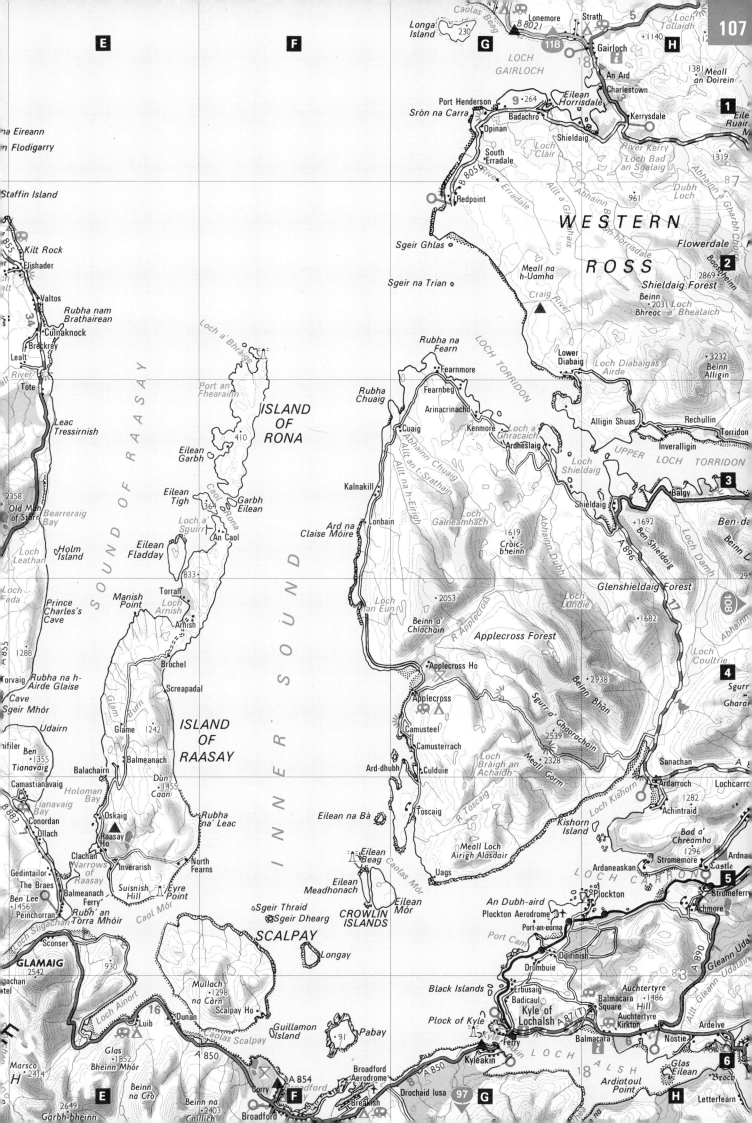

A 19 118 B C D

1 1381 Meall Doirein
2802 Beinn a' Chàisgein Mór
Dubh Loch
Beinn a' Chlaidheimh
2647 1971 Meall an t-Sithe
Breac Beag
A 832 Braemore Forest

2595 Beinn Airigh Charr

Eilean Ruaridh Mór
1319 Eilean Sùbhainn
Talladale A 832
Letterewe Forest
Letterewe

3194 Mullach Coire Mhic Fhearchair 3326
2817 Beinn Làir

2424 Groban

Loch a' Bhraoin
Meall a' Chrasgaidh 3062
Sgurr Mór 3637
Abhainn a' G

SLIOCH

A' Chailleach 3276

Meall Gorm 3109
Fannich Forest
An Coile

Flowerdale Forest
2869 Bheinn Bhealaich
Loch na h-Oidhche
Beinn an Eòin 2805
2378

Strath Lungard
Glen Grudie
R Grudie

Rhu Nòa
Meall Ghiubhais 2882

3215

Loch Garbhaig
Loch Fada
Lochan Fada

Kinlochewe Forest 1365
Beinn a' Mhùinidh 2231

Glen Tanagaidh
Abhainn Bruachaig

Beinn nan Ramh 2333
Fannich Lodge

Loch Fannic

Abhainn a' Chadh' Bhuidhe
Fionn Bheinn 3062
Meall a' Chaorainn 2313
Lochrosque Forest

Anancaun
Incheril
Heights of Kinlochewe
Kinlochewe

WESTER ROS
3232 Beinn Alligin

Ruadh-stac Mór 3313

BEINN EIGHE

Beinn Eighe National Nature Reserve

Carn a' Ghlinne 1768
Carn a' 1768

Badavanich 9
An Liathanach
Achnasheen A 832
River Bran Stra

Torridon Forest
Rechullin
Torridon Ho
LIATHACH 3456
Glen Torridon 11
A 896

Loch Clair
A' Ghairbhe
Loch Coulin
Coulin Lodge

Abhainn Dubh
1804 Carn Beag
A 890
Ledgowan Forest
Loch Gowan

1765 Carn Mhartuin
Cnap na Feola
STRA

alligin
TORRIDON
Torridon
River Torridon
Sgurr Dubh 2566
Coulin Forest
Loch Coulin

Loch Sgamhain

Scardroy

algy
Annat
Abhainn Thrail

Carn Breac 2223
Glen Carron
A 890

Loch Beannacharain

107
Ben-damph Forest
2410
Loch an Eion
Beinn Liath Mhór
Sgorr Ruadh 3142
R Lair
Craig
Glencarron Lodge
18
Moruisg 3026
Carn Gorm
Glencarron and Glenuig Forest
River Meig
Creag na h-Iolaire 2949
Bac an Eich 2787
F

Loch Damh
Beinn Damh 2957
Maol Chean-dearg 3060

Achnashellach Sta
Lair
Achnashellach Forest
Gleann Fhiodhaig

Loch na Gaoidhe

NG
Balnacra
Coulags
River Carron
Loch Dùghaill
Sgurr na Feartaig 2830
Maoile Lunndaidh 3304
2661

4
Loch Coultrie
Sgurr a' Gharaidh 2396
Glas Bheinn 2332
New Kelso
Sgurr nan Eogan 2807
Sgurr a' Chaorachain 3455
West Monar Forest
East Monar Forest

Creag a' Chaorainn
Beinn Tharsuinn 2807
Bearneas

Strathcarron
Achintee
Loch an Laoigh
Lurg Mhór 3234
Loch Monar
Monar Lodge 2272
Glen St

A 896
Kirkton
Carn a' Gheuradainn 1950
An Gead Loch
Uisge Misgeach
Glen St

8
Lochcarron
1282
Attadale
Bendronaig Lodge
Beinn Dronaig
Loch an Tachdaidh
Meallan Buidhe

Bad a' hreamha 1296
Ardnarff
Castle
8
River Attadale
Attadale Forest
Loch Cruoshie 2312
An Cruachan
Sgurr na Lapaich 3775

5
Carn nan Iomairean 1590
River Ling
Carn na Sean-lùibe
An Riabhachan 3696
3508

Stromeferry
Achmore
Ben Killilan
Loch Calavie
Aonach Buidhe 2949
East Benula Forest
Mullardoch Ho

A 890
Gleann Udalain
Sallachy
Alltan-sugh 1351
Sgùman 2883
Killilan
Cuinntich
83
Killilan Forest
2847
An Riabhachan
Loch Mullardoch
Glen Cannich
Glencannich

Camas-luinie
Glen Elchaig
River Elchaig
Carnach
Gleann Sithidh
Beinn Fhionnlaidh 3298
Toll Creagach 3475
Doire Tana

6
Ardelve
Bundalloch
Loch nan Eun
2073
Fall of Glomach
West Benula Forest
Gleann a' Choilich
Carn Eige 3880
Tom a' Chòinich 3646
Gleann nam Fiadh
2004

Dornie Castle
Broch
Keppoch
Letterfearn
Inverinate
Inverinate Forest
98
A' Ghlas-bheinn
3006
3771
Sgurr nan
Màm Sodhail 2949
Sgurr na 3401
fric

A B 19 B C 98 D

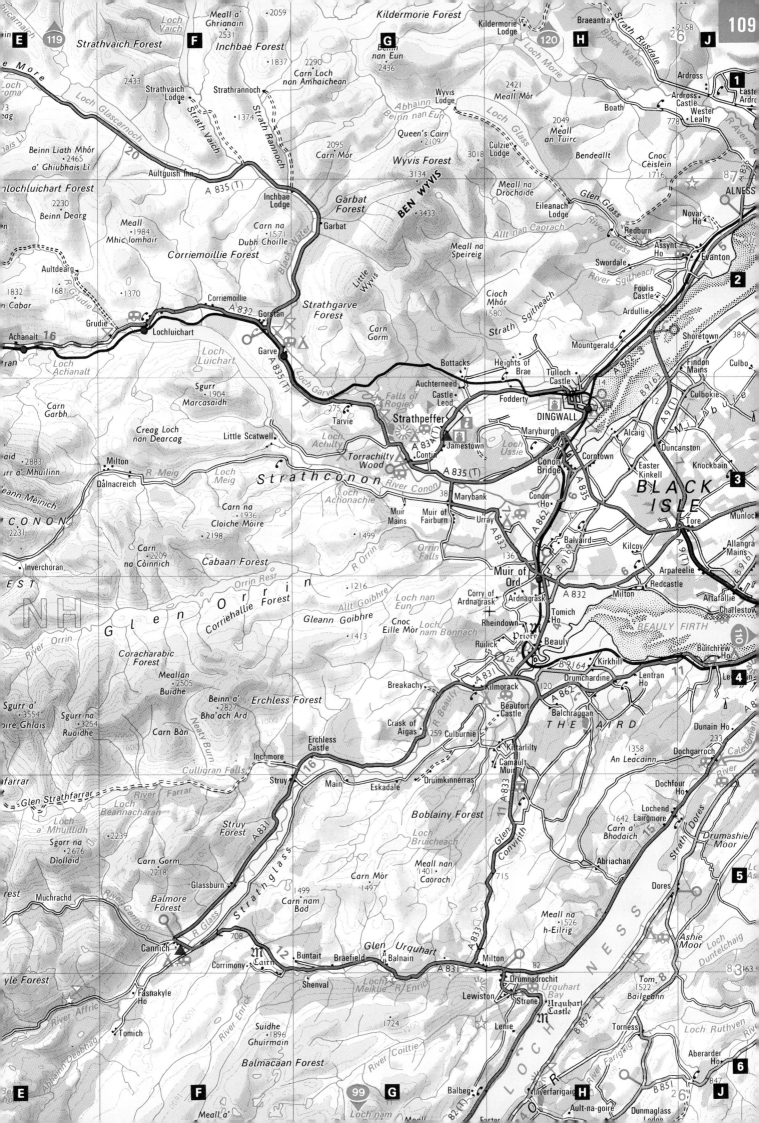

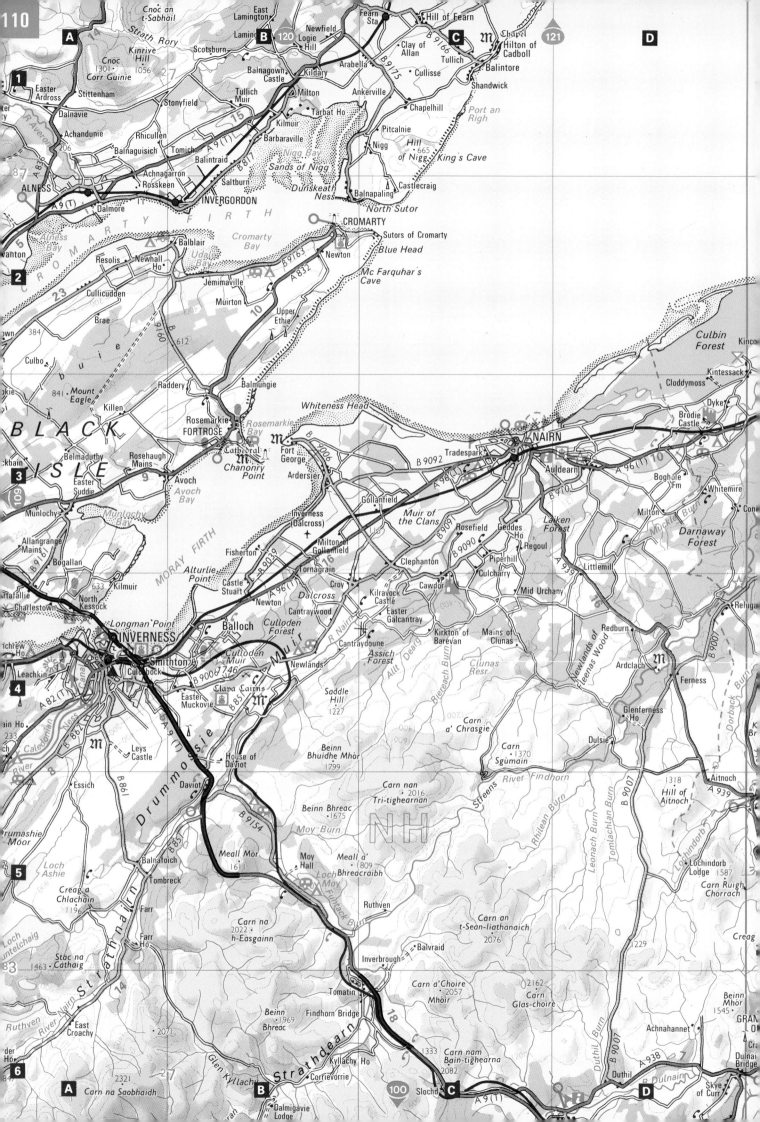

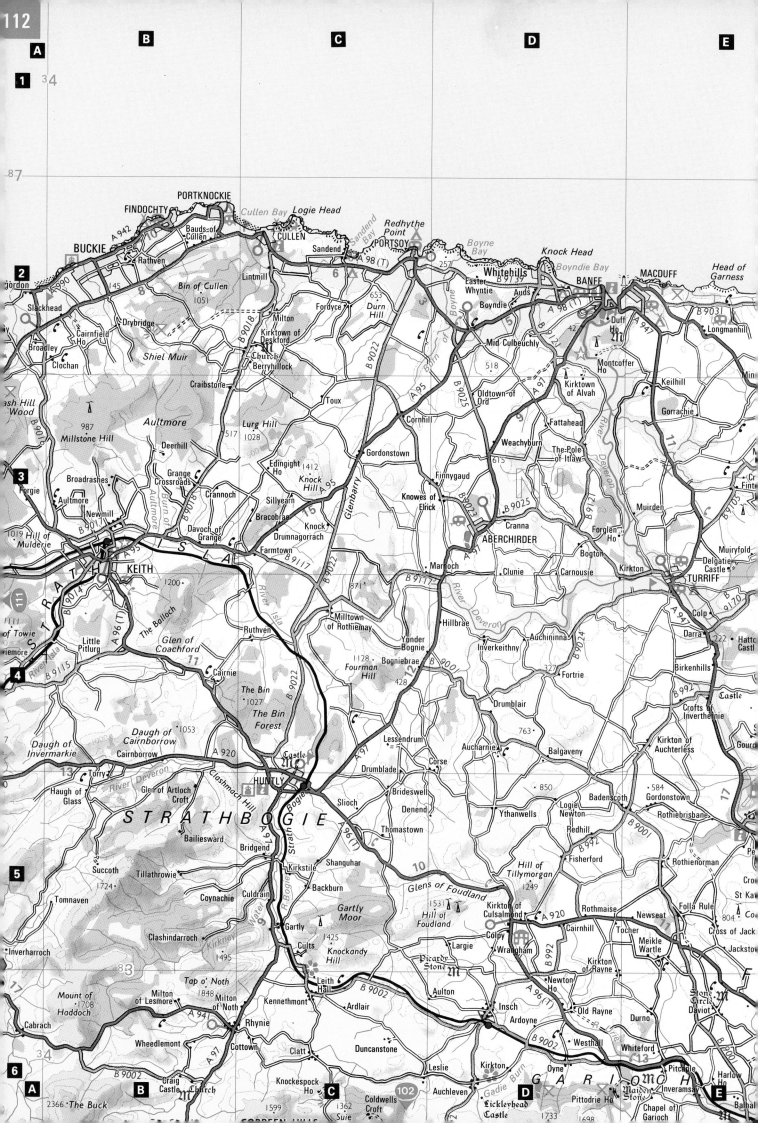

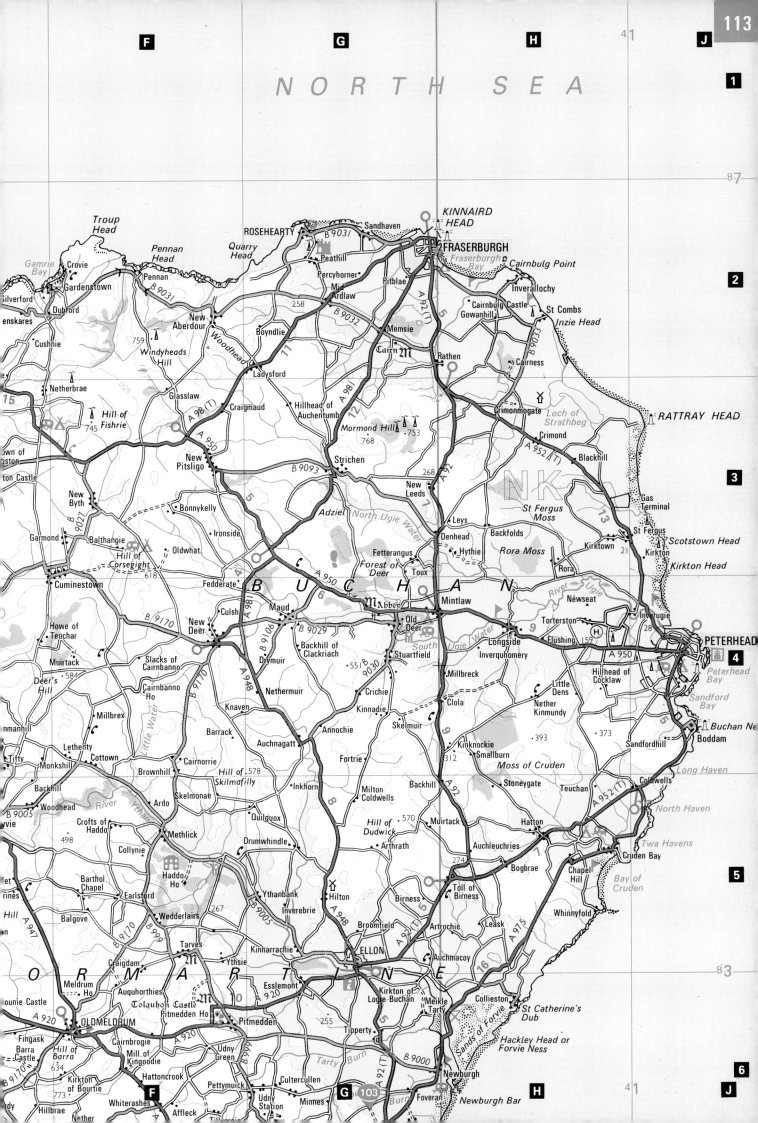

E **F** **G** **H** **J**

1 **2** **3** **4** **5** **6**

ISLE OF LEWIS

Mullach na Reidheachd 969
Liuthaid 1611
Aline Lodge
Ardvourlie
Stulaval 1901
Ullaval 2153
227
2165
Oreval
st of Harris
Meavaig
Uisgnaval Mòr 2392
Clisham
Clett Ard
1069
Seaforth Island 713

Sidhean an Airgid
A 859
18
Troimm
117
Loch Shanndabhat
Orinsay
Eishken
PARK OR PAIRC
Lemreway
Gob na Milaid
Srianach
91
Eilean Iubhard
Camas Allt nam Bearnach
247

NB

Beinn Mhòr 1874
1542
Crionaig 1532
Uisenis 1217
Mol Truisg
14

NORTH HARRIS
B 887
Mòr
Beinn Dhubh 1661
Ben Luskentyre 1532
Gob Aird an Tolmachain
Cliasmol
WEST LOCH TARBERT
Isay
Bunavoneadar
Sgaoth Aird 1829
Ardhasaig
Gillaval Glas 1547
Tarbert
Laxadale Lochs
Maaruig
Urgha
Toddun 1733
Rhenigidale
Ard Caol
Beinn a' Chaolais
Loch Trollamarig
Geo Dubh
Caiteshal 1473
Loch Claidh
L Bhrollum
Gob Rubh' Uisenis
Rubha Bhrollum
Rubh' a Bhaird
1532

SOUND OF SHIANT
Garbh Eilean
Galtachean
Cadha na Gaoidhsic
528
Eilean Mhuir
Shiant Islands
Eilean a Tighe

Luskentyre
South Harris Forest
24
Seilebost
Loch Ceann Dibig
Meavag
196
East Loch Tarbert
Carragreich
Aird Mheadhonach
Scotasay
1096
Leac Eskadale
Kyles Scalpay
Carnach
Ferry
341
Rubha Crago
Aird Riabhach
SCALPAY
Eilean Mòr a' Bhàigh
Eilean Glas

 S
R
R
A
H
NG
SOUTH HARRIS
1267
An Coileach
Ardvey
Likisto
Drinishader
Ceann-na-Cleithe
Lackalee
Grosebay
Geocrab
Kyles Stockinish
Cluer
Plocrapool Point
Plocrapool
Scadabay
Loch Grosebay
Rubha Bhocaig

Beacravik
Bràigh-nam-bàgh
Flodabay
Manish
Aird Mhànais
Stockinish Island
Ardvey
Finsbay
Quidnish
Loch Flodabay
Rubha Quidnish
Loch Finsbay
Lingarabay
Lingarabay Island
urch
Vallay
NISH NT

HEBRIDES OR WESTERN ISLES

THE LITTLE MINCH

2½ hrs
2 hrs
2 hrs

Fladda-chùain 83
Sgeir nam Maol

Eilean Trodday

RUBHA HUNISH
Loch Hunish
Tulm Bay
The Aird
An t-Iasgair
106
Kilmaluag
Lub Score
Monument
Camas Mòr
Bornesketaig
Cairidh nan Òb
Kilmuir
Kilvaxter
Balgown
Suidh'a'Mhinn
Kilbride Point
Linicro
Totscore
A 855
14
87
Mea
17
Bio
Buie
Buio

WATERNISH POINT
An Càmastac
Healaval
Eilean Iosal
Eilean Creagach
Ascrib Islands
W A T
Ben Geary 931
Geary
Ard Beag
Trumpan
106
Loch Losait
Ardmore Point
Halistra
Gillen
Idrigill
Uig Bay
Ru Chorachan
LOCH SNIZORT
Earlish
A 856
Balnaknock
River Rha
River Conon
Poll na

E **F** **G** **H** **J**

RONA AND SULA SGEIR

1

Lisgear Mhór

Rona

Lòba Sheir

Gealldruig Mhór

2

HW

Sula
Sgeir

Rona lies about 44 miles or 70 km NNE of the Butt of Lewis NB 5166

J   17   K   18   L

09

D

3

NA

Poll
Gainmhich

Campay

Loch Carloway

Floday

Little
Bernera

Creag
Mhór

Broch

Harsgeir

4

94

WEST
LOCH ROAG

Gallan Head

Bosta

Croir

Tobson

265

Camas Geodhachan
an Duilisg

Aird
Uig

Geodha nan Calmàn

EAST LOCH ROAG

Geodha Nasavig

Valtos

Pabay
Mór

Vacsay

Breaclete

GREAT
BERNERA

To

Fiavig B'agh

670

Kneep

Hacklete

Kirkibost

Sgeir Fiavig Tarris

Forsnaval

Miavaig

Reef

Vuia
Mór

Barraglom

Totarol

Crowlista

Timsgarry

Eilean
Kearstay

4

Camas
Uig

Floday

Vuia Beag

Crulivig

Stan
St

Ard More
Mangersta

Ardroil

Carishader

Geshader

Linsha

Loch
Scaslavat

1404

Suainaval

LOCH ROAG

840

Mangersta

Teahaval

Loch
Tungavat

Aird Fenish

Cleite
Leathann

Enaclete

Staca Leathann

Islivig

Tarain

Loch Grùnavat

Gisla R

Gisla

Aird Brenish

Mealisval

5

92

Brenish

Camas a' Mhoil

Mealista

1625

Laival a
Tuath

Loch
Chaolartan

1303

Loch
Fuaroil

Loch
Morsgail

Mealasta

Beinn
Mheadhonach

Griomaval

Maghannan

Mealasta
Island

Loch
Crò Criosdaig

Loch
Coirigerod

Loch Benisval

Loch
Tamanavay

Morsgail
Forest

Kearstay

Gob na h-
Airde Móire

Loch
Resort

1008

Beinn
a' Bhoth

6

09

Bràigh Mór

Sron
Romul

1012

SCARP

994

Taran Mór

969

Mullach na
Reidheachd

1611

Liuthaid

Manish

A   09   B   114   C   D

Hushinish

1603

1901

Aline
Lodge

Butt of Lewis
Cladach an Eilein
Cunnda
Eoropie
Five Penny Ness
Lionel
Port of Ness
Port Skigersta
Cross Sands
Habost
Swainbost
Aird Dell
Dell
Cross
Ness
Skigersta
Meall Geal
Toa Galson
A 857
Glen Cross
Cuiashader
Cladach Cuiashader
Galson
Roinn a' Bhuic
Melbost Borve
Dell River
Cellar Head
Five Penny Borve
High Borve
Ben Dell
Rubha Bhlanisgaidh
South Galson River
Loch Langavat
Cladach Dibadale
Rubha Leathann
Shader
Steinacleit
Borve River
Cladach Dibadale
Aird Barvas
Ballantrushal
520 Diaval
Sguinean nan Creagan Briste
Rubh' a' Bhiogair
Loch Mòr Sandavat
Rinn Druim Tallig
Labost
Brue
Barvas
Abhainn Geiraha
bh' an Dùnain
Arnol
Rubha Caol
Bragar
Loch Urrahag
813 Muirneag
New Tolsta
386
Bay
Shawbost
River Arnol
A 858
North Tolsta
Tolsta Head
Dalbeg
19
Gleann Mòr Barvas 12
Loch Breivat
Abhainn Ghriais
Glen Tolsta
Dalmore
459 Beinn Bragar
Gleann Bhruthadail
A 857
Loch Sgeireach Mòr
Port Bun a' Ghlinne
rloway
NB
Glen Bragar
Loch na Scaravat
Lacastal
13
Griais
Creag Fhraoch
olais
459
955 Beinn Mholach
Loch Mòr an Stàirr
Abhainn Chuil
Bac
Sgeir Leathann
Loch Laxavat Ard
Loch nan Stèarnag
Col
asclete
Gob Rubha Bhatasgeir
BROAD BAY OR LOCH A' TUATH
Rubha an Tiumpain
Col Uarach
Tràigh Chuil
460
Cnoc Amhlaigh
New Lands
Port Mholair
Callanish
River Laxdale
Grianan
Aird Thunga
B 895
Tunga
Sròn Ruadh
Shulishader
Aird Bholair
Bagh Phort
Stone Circle
Garynahine
Newmarket
Tràigh Mhealaboist
Seisiadar
Laxdale
STORNOWAY
Stornoway Aerodrome
Garrabost
Rubha na Greine
avat
A 858
Greeta River or R Creed
Lewis Castle College
Melbost
Aignish
EYE PENINSULA
Rubha nam Bàirneach
B 8011
A 858
Sandwick
A 866
Knock
Pabail Uarach
Bagh Phabail
Pabail Iarach
Lochganvich
732 Eitshal
Arnish Moor
Holm
Gob Shilldinish
Stac Shuardail
288 Bayble Hill
Rubh' Dubh
avat
Achmore
14
Rubh' a' Bhàigh Uaine
Gob na Geige
Roineval
A 859
B 897
Loch Uraval
Loch Orasay
STORNOWAY to
Ullapool.................3½ hrs
Leurbost
Grimshader
Ben Casgro
Raerinish Point
Loch Thota Bridein
Loch nam Falcag
Soval Lodge
Crossbost
Ranish
HEBRIDES OR WESTERN ISLES
Loch Trealaval
396 Trealaval
Keose
Barkin Isles
Tabhaidh Mhór
Loch Airigh na h' Airde
12
Eilean Chaluim Chille
Eilean Orasaidh
Laxay
kintarvie
Balallan
Loch Erisort
Cromore
Eilean Thòraidh
Loch Strandavat
Shiltenish
Kershader
Caversta
Marvig
Rubha na Creige Móire
THE MINCH
Arivruaich
Habost
B 8060
Malasgair
Seaforth Head
Loch Sgibacleit
Loch nan Eilean
Calbost
A 859
Aird an Troim
Glenside
Rubha Iosal
Sidhean an Airgid
Loch Shanndabhat
Gravir
Loch Odhairn
Kebock Head

PARK OR
Orinsay
Eishken
Lemreway

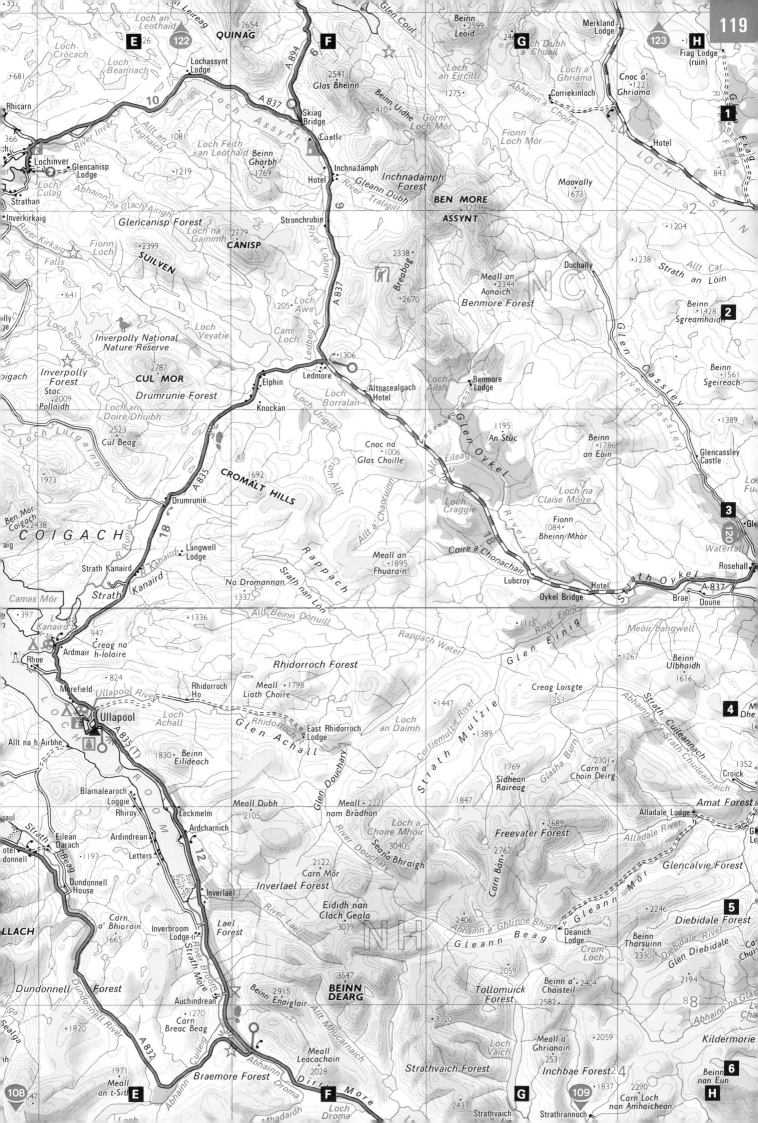

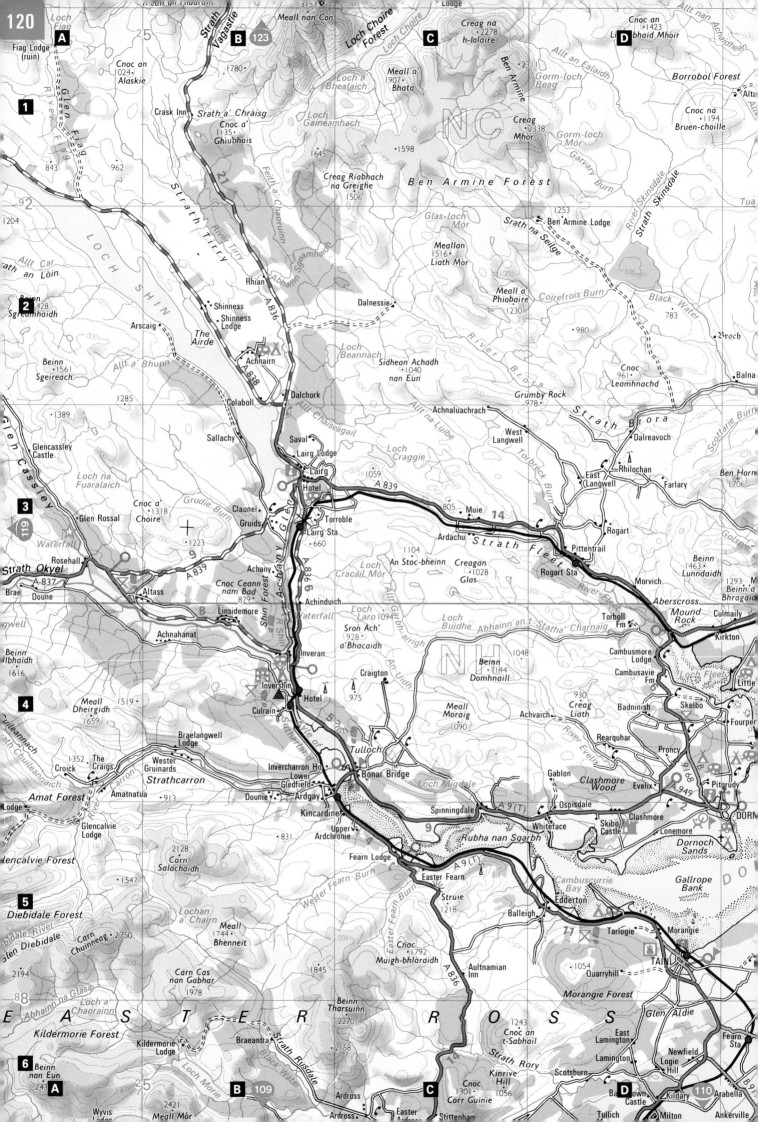

E
F
124
G
125
H

Dunbeath
Dunbeath Bay
Dunbeath Castle

•928
Knockally
Ramscraigs
Borgue •892
Newport
An Dùn
Langwell Ho
20
Ceann Leathad nam Bò
Berriedale

1587
Maiden Pap
•1434
Choc-Coire na Feannа
•1699
Cnoc an Eireannaich
2313
Morven
2055
Scaraben
Meall na •1301 Caorach
ND

•912
Borrobol Lodge
•859
A 897
na Frithe
Creag •1271 m Fiadh
Loch Ascaig

Strath of Kildonan

Kinbace Burn
Suisgill Burn
Kildonan Burn
•1582
Creag •1819 Scalabsdale

826
Kildonan Lodge
17
Beinn •1365 Dubhain

•1026
Cnoc na Maoile
Wag
Lāngwell Forest
Aultibea
Langwell Water

•1387
Langwell Ho

Boch-ailean
Ousdale

92

•163
•Craggie

Cnoc •1134 Meadhonach

Craggie Water
Helmsdale

Torrish
Kilphedir
•1321
Ord Point

Meallan •1512 Liath Beag

Beinn •2060 Dhorain
•1581
•1940

Eldrable •1338 Hill
West Helmsdale
Helmsdale

Glen Sletdale
Glen Loth

Gartymore
Portgower

•1592
•1765
1294
Col-bheinn

11
Lothmore

Sron Rubha na Gaoithe

Gordonbush
Loch Brora

A 9 (T)
Lothbeg
Lothbeg Point

West Clyne
730
Clynelish

Cagar •1239 Feosaig
Doll
Brora

Backies
9
Broch m
Dunrobin Castle
Golspie

1

2

3

4

FIRTH
OCH

Tarbat Ness
Wilkhaven

5

Portmahomack

Rockfield

Inver
Tarrel
Arboll
Lochslin

eness nds
Eye

88

Rhynie
B 9165
Geanies Ho

Hill of Fearn
m
Chapel
Hilton of Cadboll
Tullich
B 9166
ullisse
Balintore
Shandwick

E
F
111
G
H

6

32
32

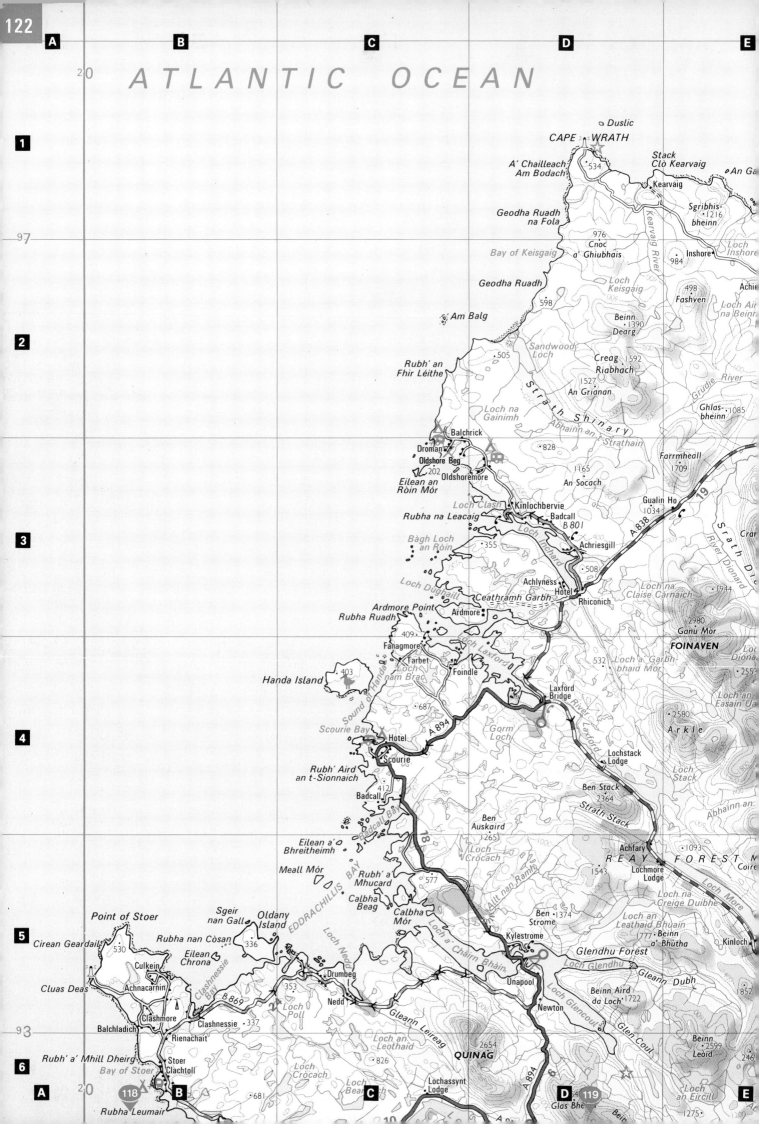

A **B** **C** **D** **E**

ATLANTIC OCEAN

20

97

Duslic
CAPE WRATH
A' Chailleach
Am Bodach
•534
Stack
Clò Kearvaig
An Ga
Kearvaig
Sgribhis-
•1216 bheinn
Geodha Ruadh
na Fola
976
Cnoc
a' Ghiubhais
Inshore
Loch Inshore
Bay of Keisgaig
984
498
Fashven
Loch Air
Loch
na Beinn
Keisgaig
Achie
598
Beinn •1390
Dearg
Geodha Ruadh
Creag 1592
Riabhach
1527
Am Balg
•505
Strath Shinary
Grudie River
Rubh' an
Fhir Léithe
Abhainn an t-Strathain
An Grianan
Ghlas-
•1085
bheinn
Loch na
Gainimh
•828
Farrmheall
Balchrick
Droman
•1165
•709
Oldshore Beg
An Socach
Gualin Ho
202
Oldshoremore
1034
A 838
Strath Di
Eilean an Ròin Mór
Loch Clash
Kinlochbervie
19
Rubha na Leacaig
Badcall
Crar
B 801
Achriesgill
Bàgh Loch
an Ròin
•355
•508
Loch na
Claise Carnaich
1944
Loch Dughaill
Achlyness
Hotel
Loch Inchard
Rhiconich
2980
Ardmore Point
Ceathramh Garbh
Ganu Mór
Rubha Ruadh
Ardmore
FOINAVEN
Loch
409
Loch Laxford
Diona
Fanagmore
532
Loch a' Garbh-
bhaid Mór
255
Tarbet
Loch
nam Bràc
Foindle
Loch an
Easain Ua
Handa Island
403
2580
Arkle
Sound of Handa
•687
Laxford
Bridge
Scourie Bay
A 894
Gorm
Loch
Lochstack
Lodge
Loch
Stack
Hotel
Scourie
Rubh' Aird
an t-Sionnaich
Ben Stack
2364
412
Badcall
Strath Stack
Badcall Bay
18
Ben Auskaird
Achfary
•1093
Eilean a'
Bhreitheimh
1265
1543
REAY FOREST M
Lochmore
Lodge
Coire
Meall Mór
Rubh' a'
Mhucard
577
Loch
Cròcach
Loch na
Creige Duibhe
Allt nan Ramh
Calbha Beag
Ben
Stroma
1374
Loch an
Leathaid Bhuain
Point of Stoer
Sgeir
nan Gall
Oldany
Island
Calbha
Mór
Kylestrome
•777 Beinn
a' Bhutha
Kinloch
Cirean Geardail
Rubha nan Còsan
336
EDDRACHILLIS BAY
Loch Nedd
Loch a' Chàirn Bhàin
Glendhu Forest
530
Eilean
Chrona
Unapool
Loch Glendhu
Gleann Dubh
Cluas Deas
Culkein
Achnacarnin
Drumbeg
Newton
Beinn Aird
da Loch 1722
1852
Clashnessie
B 869
353
Nedd
Gleann Leireag
Loch Glencoul
Clashmore
Balchladich
Rienachait
Clashnessie •337
Loch
Poll
A 894
6
Beinn
•2599
Leoid
93
Stoer
Loch an
Leathaid
2654
246
Rubh' a' Mhill Dheirg
Clachtoll
Loch
Cròcach
•826
QUINAG
Lochassynt
Lodge
Loch
an Eircill
Bay of Stoer
1275
A 20 118 **B** 681 **C** Loch Bean **D** 119 **E**
Rubha Leumair
Glas Bhe
Bein
10

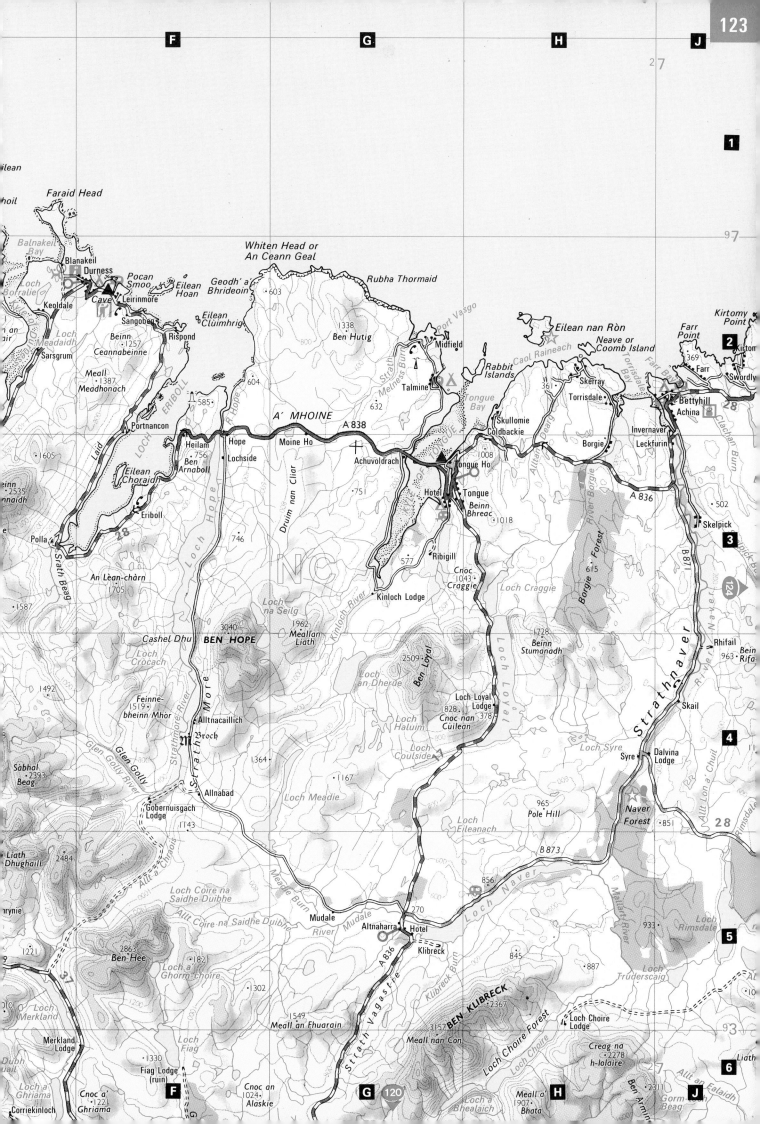

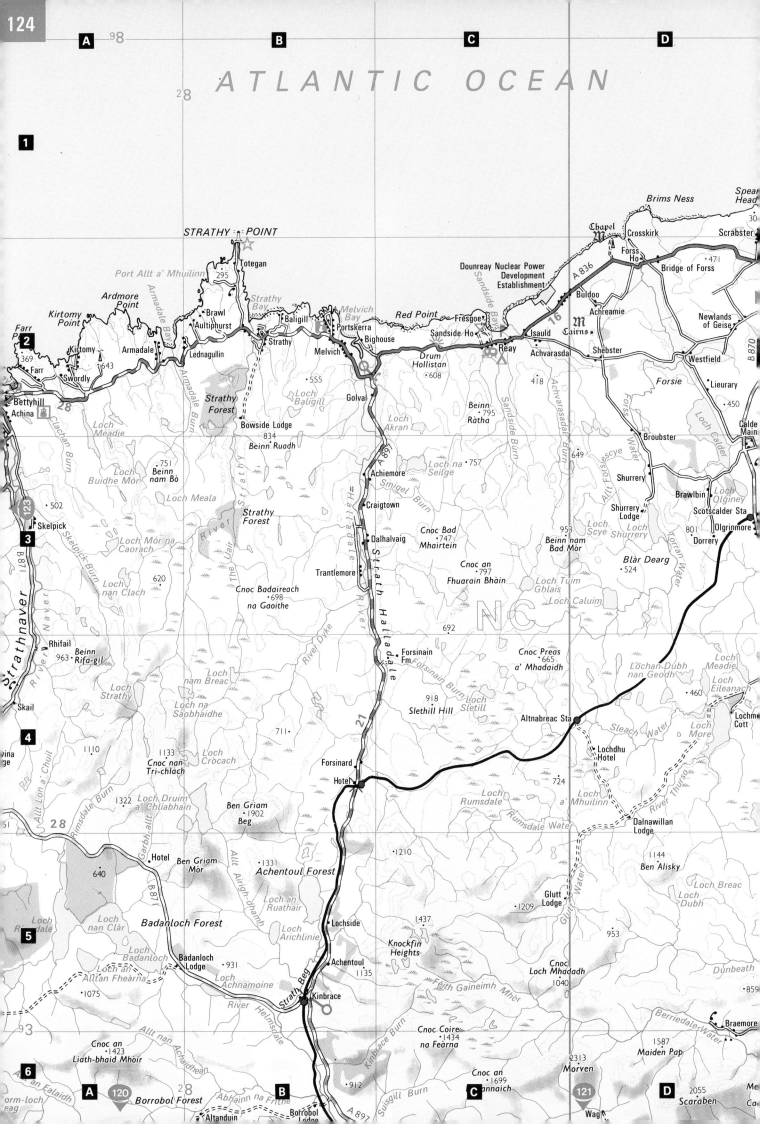

ATLANTIC OCEAN

Brims Ness
Spear Head

Chapel
Crosskirk
Scrabster
Forss Ho
Dounreay Nuclear Power
Development
Establishment
A 836
Bridge of Forss
•471
Buldoo
Achreamie
Newlands
of Geise
16
Red Point
Fresgoe
Sandside Ho
Isauld
M Cairns
Shebster
Westfield
Achvarasdal
Forsie
B 870
STRATHY POINT
Totegan
295
Port Allt a' Mhuilinn
Strathy
Bay
Melvich
Bay
Sandside Bay
Reay
418
Lieurary
•450
Ardmore Point
Brawl
Aultiphurst
Baligill
Portskerra
Bighouse
Drum
Hollistan
•608
Forss Water
Broubster
Calde
Main
Kirtomy
Point
Armadale Bay
Strathy
Melvich
Golval
Beinn
•795
Ràtha
Allt Forsiescye
Loch Calder
Kirtomy
Armadale
Lednagullin
•555
Loch
Baligill
Loch
Akran
Sandside Burn
649
Achvarasdal Burn
Shurrery
Brawlbin
Loch
Olginey
Farr
P
•369
•1643
Loch Meadie
Strathy
Forest
Achiemore
Loch na
Seilge
•757
Loch
Scye
Shurrery
Lodge
Loch
Shurrery
Scotscalder Sta
801
Olgrinmore
Farr
Swordly
Bowside Lodge
834
Beinn Ruadh
953
Beinn nam
Bad Mór
Dorrery
Bettyhill
Achina
Clachan Burn
Loch Meadie
Beinn
•751
nam Bò
Craigtown
Smigel Burn
Cnoc Bad
•747
Mhairtein
Blàr Dearg
•524
Torran Water
Skelpick
123
•502
Loch
Buidhe Mór
Loch Meala
Strathy
Forest
Dalhalvaig
Cnoc an
•797
Fhuarain Bhàin
Loch Tuim
Ghlais
NC
River Naver
1189
Skelpick Burn
Loch Mór na
Caorach
The Uair
River Strathy
Strath Halladale
Trantlemore
Loch Caluim
Strathnaver
620
Loch
nan Clach
Cnoc Badaireach
•698
na Gaoithe
River Dyke
692
Cnoc Preas
•665
a' Mhadaidh
Lochan Dubh
nan Geodh
Loch
Meadie
Rhifail
963
Beinn
Rifa-gil
Loch
nam Breac
Forsinain
Fm
Forsinain Burn
•460
Loch
Eileanach
Skail
Loch
Strathy
Loch na
Saobhaidhe
918
Slethill Hill
Loch
Sletill
Altnabreac Sta
Sleach Water
Lochm
Cott
711•
Halladale River
Loch
More
1110
1133
Loch
Cròcach
Cnoc nan
Tri-chlach
21
Lochdhu
Hotel
724
Allt Ion a' Chuil
Rimsdale Burn
1322
Loch Druim
a' Chliabhain
Ben Griam
•1902
Beg
Forsinard
Hotel
Loch
Rumsdale
Rumsdale Water
River Thurso
Dalnawillan
Lodge
1144
Ben Alisky
51
28
Hotel
640
Ben Griam
Mór
B 871
•1331
Achentoul Forest
•1210
Glutt Water
Loch
a' Mhuilinn
Glutt
Lodge
1209
Loch Breac
Loch
Dubh
Badanloch Forest
Loch
nan Clàr
Loch
Badanloch
Badanloch
Lodge
•931
Allt Airigh-dhamh
Loch an
Ruathair
Loch
Arichlinie
Lochside
1437
Knockfin
Heights
Fèith Gaineimh Mhór
Cnoc
Loch Mhadadh
1040
953
Dunbeath
•859
Loch
R sdale
Loch an
Alltan Fheàrna
•1075
Loch
Achnamoine
River Helmsdale
Strath Beg
Achentoul
1135
Kinbrace
Cnoc Coire
•1434
na Fearna
Kinbrace Burn
Suisgill Burn
Berriedale Water
Braemore
•93
Cnoc an
•1423
Liath-bhaid Mhóir
Allt nan Achaidhean
•912
Cnoc an
•1699
annaich
2313
Morven
1587
Maiden Pap
2055
Scaraben

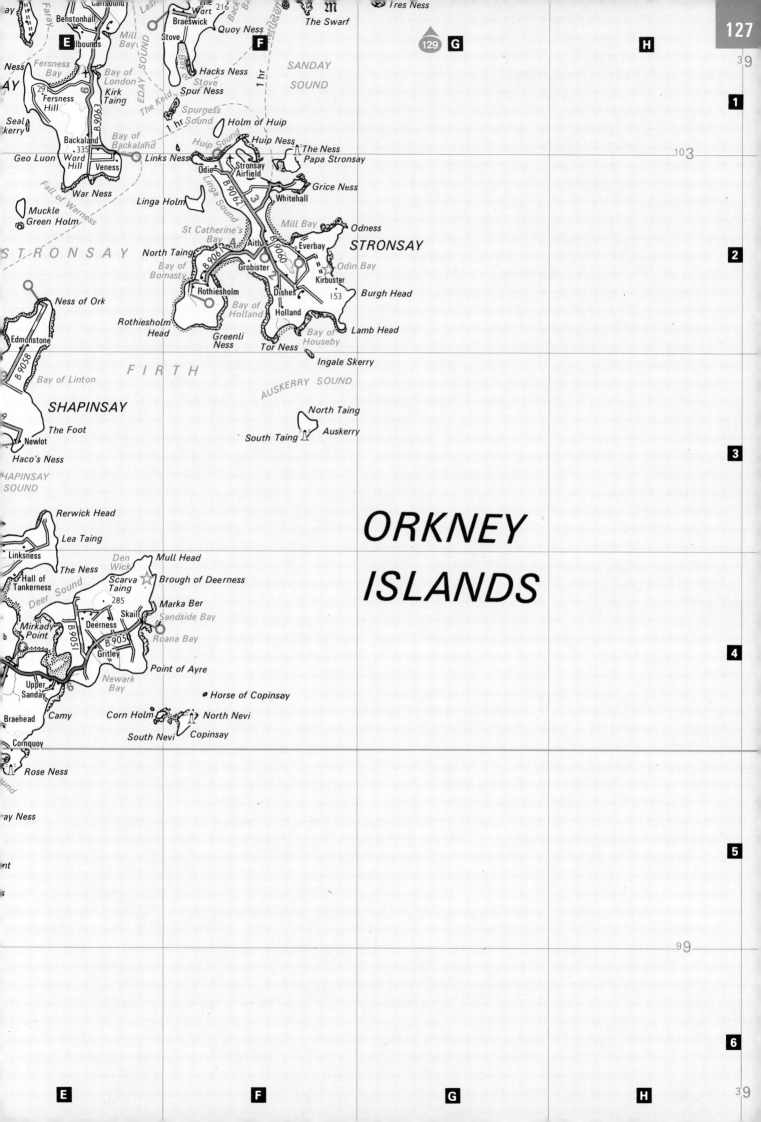

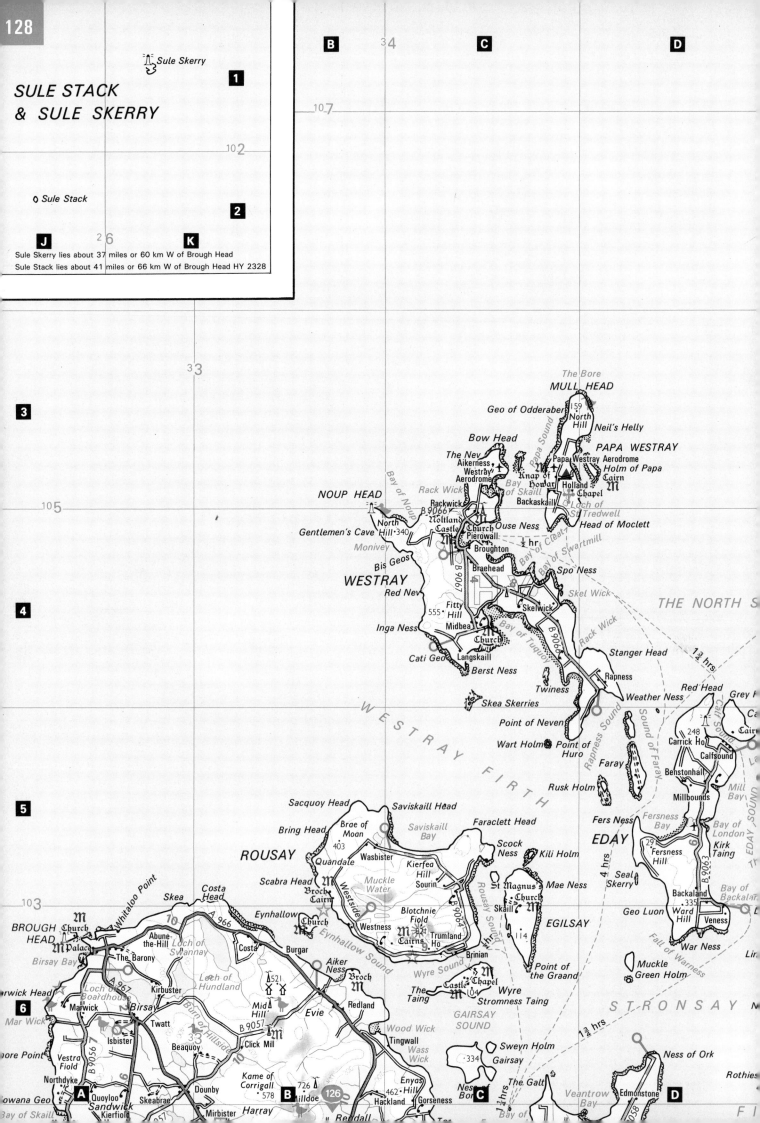

SULE STACK & SULE SKERRY

Sule Skerry

Sule Stack

Sule Skerry lies about 37 miles or 60 km W of Brough Head
Sule Stack lies about 41 miles or 66 km W of Brough Head HY 2328

The Bore
MULL HEAD
Geo of Odderaberry
North Hill
Neil's Helly
Bow Head
PAPA WESTRAY
The Nev
Aikerness
Westray
Aerodrome
Papa Westray Aerodrome
Holm of Papa
Knap of Howar
Holland
Cairn
NOUP HEAD
Rackwick
Chapel
B.9066
Noltland Castle
Backaskaill
Loch of St Tredwell
Ouse Ness
Gentlemen's Cave
Church
Head of Moclett
North Hill ·340
Pierowall
Monivey
Broughton
½ hr
Bay of Swartmill
WESTRAY
Braehead
Spo Ness
Bis Geos
Skel Wick
Red Nev
THE NORTH S
Fitty Hill
Skelwick
Rack Wick
555·
Bay of Tuquoy
B.9066
Inga Ness
Midbea
Stanger Head
Church
1¾ hrs
Cati Geo
Langskaill
Rapness
Red Head
Grey
Berst Ness
Twiness
Weather Ness
248
Carrick Ho
Ca
Skea Skerries
Cairn
Point of Neven
WESTRAY FIRTH
Calfsound
Wart Holm
Point of Huro
Benstonhall
Faray
Millbounds
Rusk Holm
Fers Ness
Fersness Bay
Bay of London
EDAY
Fersness Hill
Sacquoy Head
Saviskaill Head
Kirk Taing
Bring Head
Brae of Moan
Saviskaill Bay
Faraclett Head
Seal Skerry
29
ROUSAY
403
Wasbister
Scock Ness
Kili Holm
Mae Ness
Geo Luon
Backaland
·335
Bay of Backala
Quandale
Kierfea Hill
St Magnus's Church
Ward Hill
Veness
Scabra Head
Muckle Water
Sourin
Skaill
EGILSAY
Broch Cairn
Blotchnie Field
War Ness
Whitaloo Point
Costa Head
Skea
A.966
Eynhallow
Westside
Trumland Ho
Point of the Graand
Muckle Green Holm
BROUGH HEAD
Church
Eynhallow Sound
Westness
Cairns
Brinian
Abune-the-Hill
Loch of Swannay
Costa
Burgar
Wyre Sound
STRONSAY
Palace
The Barony
Aiker Ness
Broch
Chapel
Birsay Bay
Loch of Hundland
Redland
Castle
104
Wyre
The Taing
Stromness Taing
arwick Head
Loch of Boardhouse
A.967
521
Evie
GAIRSAY SOUND
Kirbuster
Ness of Ork
Marwick
Birsay
Mid Hill
B.9057
Wood Wick
Sweyn Holm
Twatt
Click Mill
Tingwall
Wass Wick
·334
Gairsay
Rothies
ore Point
Isbister
33
Beaquoy
The Galt
Vestra Fiold
Kame of Corrigall
726
·578
Enyas Hill
462·
Veantrow Bay
Edmonstone
Northdyke
Quoyloo
Skeabrae
Dounby
Hackland
Gorseness
Ness Bo
owana Geo
Sandwick
Kierfiold
Mirbister
Harray
Rendall
Bay of Skaill
FI

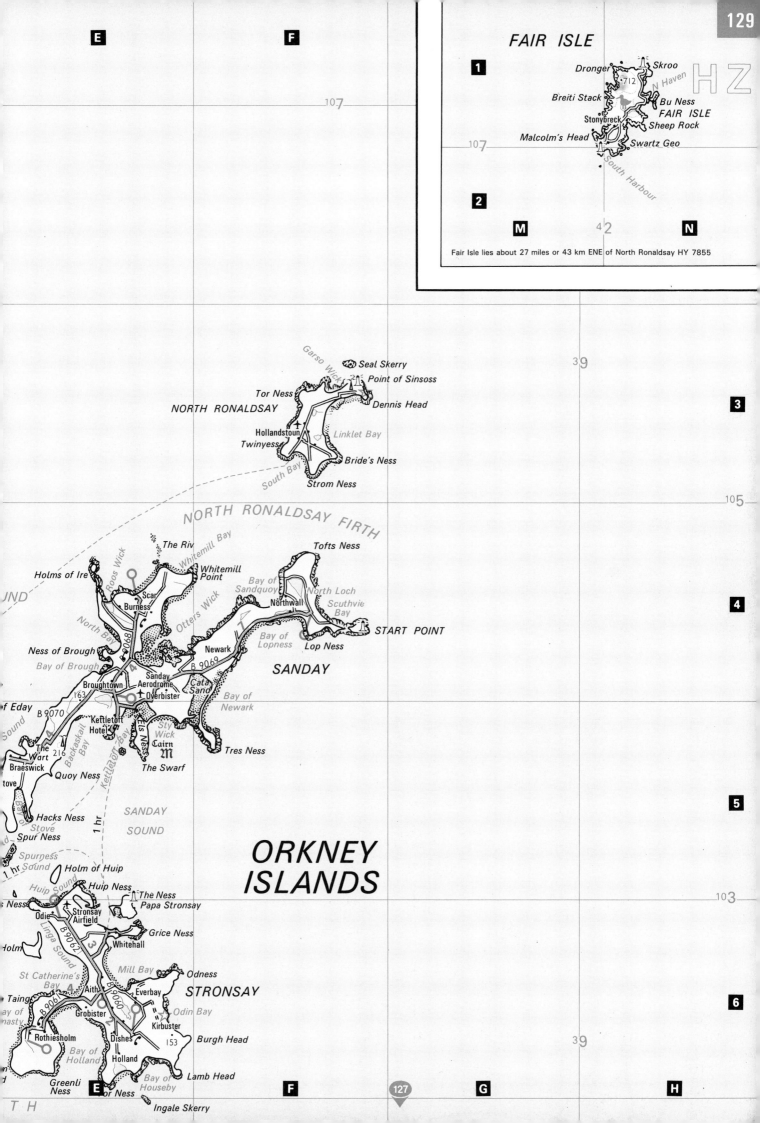

A 40 B C D

1
119

Uyea 23
Burrier Wick
Fugla Ness
South Wick

Hevdadale Head
Lang Clodie Wick

Gruna Stack
The Faither   Turls Head
Muckle Ossa   351 Ketligill
Heillia Head
Ockran Head   Burries
Ness

1475
Ronas
Hill

2

South Head
Whalwick Taing   Gluss
Water
Head of Stanshi   Hamnavoe
Grind of the Navir   Ure   Heylor
Scraada   Scarff   567
ESHA NESS   Sae   Braehoulland   B 9078   Burnside   A 970   Urafirth
Breck
205   Tangwick   Brae Wick
The Bruddans   Hillswick
Isle of Stenness   Stenness   Ness of
Skerry of Eshaness   Hillswick
Dore Holm   The Drongs
Baa Taing

Isle of Nibon

3
114

┌───┐
│ Foula lies about 14 miles or 22 km WSW of Wats Ness HU 1750 │
│   │
│ ## FOULA   **1**   │
│   │
│   Da Logat   Strem Ness   │
│   • Harrier   114   │
│   The Kame   │
│ Da Scrodhurdins   373   Head o'   │
│   The   Ham   da Taing   │
│ Wester Hoevdi   Sneug   FOULA   │
│   Hametoun   **2** │
│   Wick of   │
│   Mucklabrek   │
│   Hesti Geo   │
│   Hellabrick's Wick   │
│   South Ness   │
│   L H T   40   │
└───┘

ST MAGNUS   Lang Head
BAY

Egilsay

Turvalds He
Erne Stack

Strom Ness

4

MUCKLE ROE

Murbie Stacks Little-

Ve Skerries   Swarbacks Head
Vementry   Cairn
Cribbie   298
North Ness
Fogla Skerry   285   PAPA STOUR
Virda   Isle of
Field   West Burrafirth   Gruna
Biggings   West
Burrafirth   Brindister
Sound of Papa   Holm of Melby   Noonsbrough
Melby Ho   Garth   Unifirth
Quilva Taing   Sandness   Sulma
Water

SHETLAND

Pund Head   817   Burga
Sandness   Water   Loch of
Hill   Voxterby
Bay of Deepdale   400
5

ISLANDS

Dale   T
Mu Ness   Burn of Dale
567   A 971
Voe of Dale   Stourbrough   246
Wats Ness   Hill   Bridge of Walls   Effirth
Stanydale
Skarpigarth   Mid Walls   Se
Burraland   Walls
Braga Ness   Gruting
Vaila   Seli Voe
Sound   Garder
Uskie Geo   Vaila
Hall   Ward of   355
Culswick   Goss
Vaila   268   390   Culswick   Wate
6   Strom Ness   Brock   Easter
Housa   Skeld
The Nev   Water   Wester
Skeld
Westerwick   Silwick
Giltarump   West Moulie Geo   Skeld
Wester Wick   Ness
Sil Wick
114

A 40 B C D

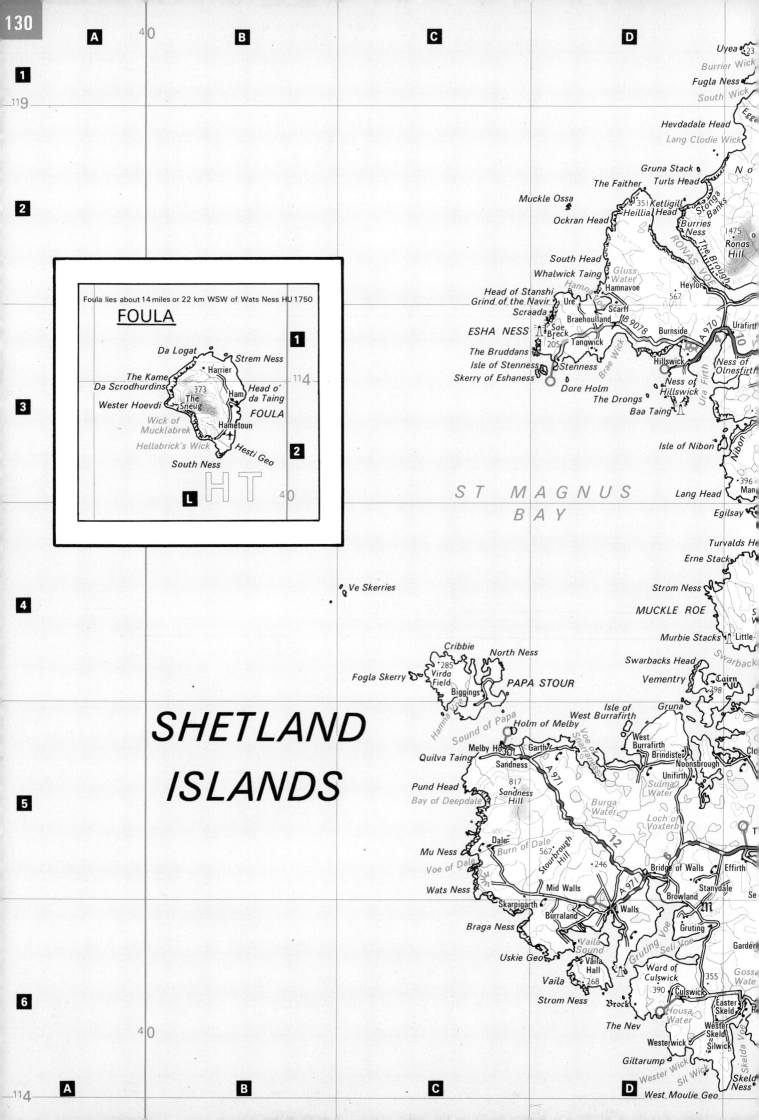

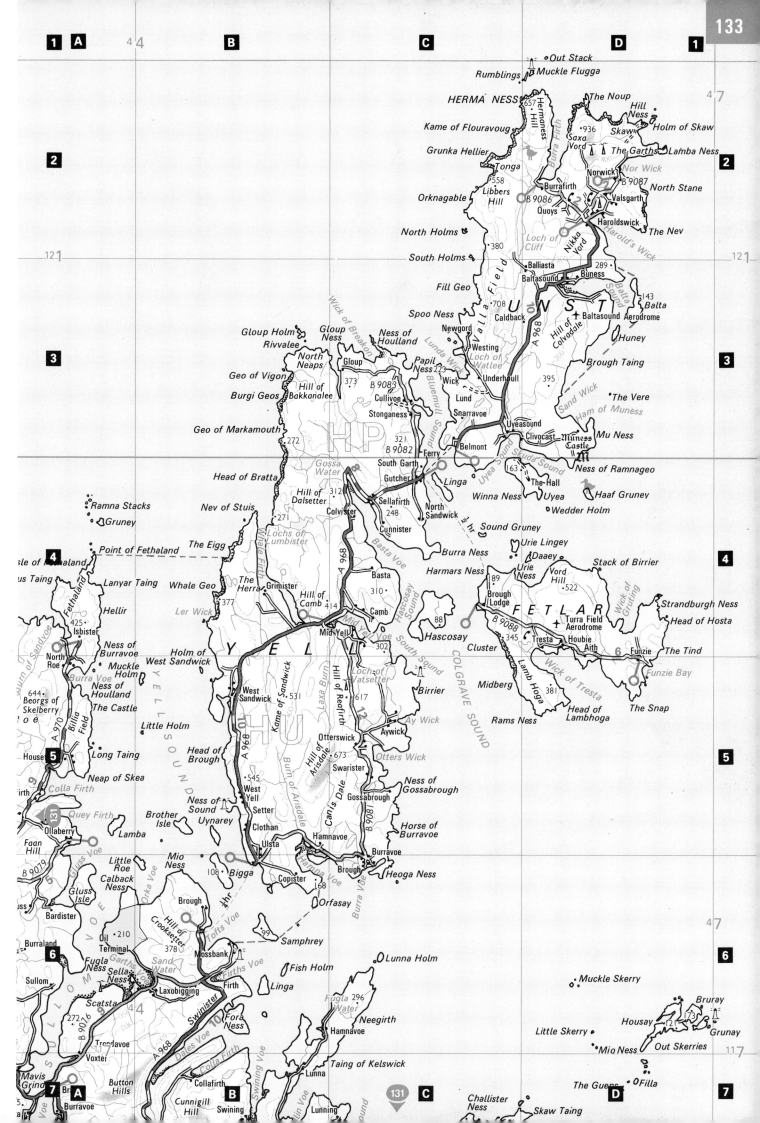

Principal Airports

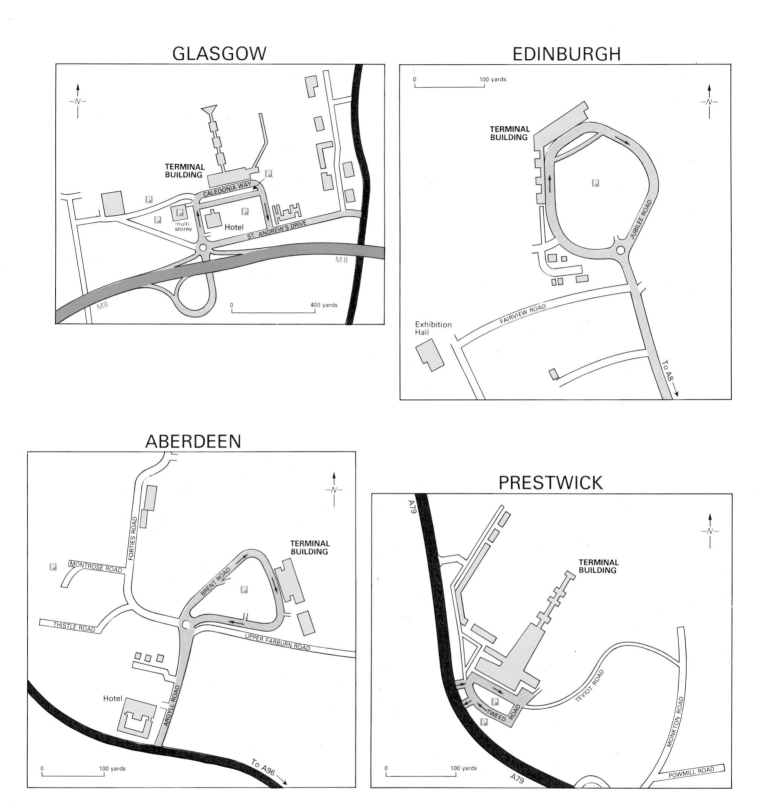

GLASGOW

TERMINAL BUILDING

CALEDONIA WAY

P

P

P

P

multi-storey

Hotel

ST. ANDREW'S DRIVE

M8

M8

0   400 yards

EDINBURGH

0   100 yards

TERMINAL BUILDING

P

JUBILEE ROAD

FAIRVIEW ROAD

Exhibition Hall

To A8

ABERDEEN

FORTIES ROAD

P

MONTROSE ROAD

BRENT ROAD

TERMINAL BUILDING

P

THISTLE ROAD

UPPER FARBURN ROAD

ARGYLL ROAD

Hotel

0   100 yards

To A96

PRESTWICK

A79

TERMINAL BUILDING

P

TWEED ROAD

TEVIOT ROAD

MONKTON ROAD

P

A79

POWMILL ROAD

0   100 yards

Ferry Ports

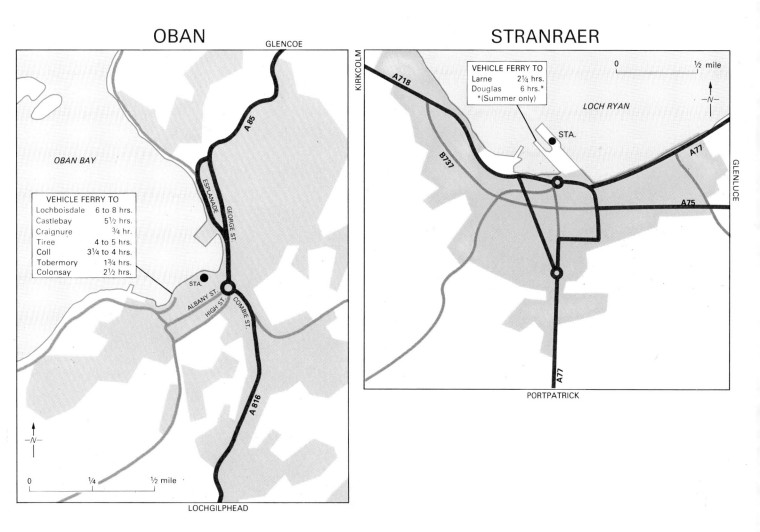

OBAN

GLENCOE

A 85

OBAN BAY

ESPLANADE

GEORGE ST.

VEHICLE FERRY TO
Lochboisdale	6 to 8 hrs.
Castlebay	5½ hrs.
Craignure	¾ hr.
Tiree	4 to 5 hrs.
Coll	3¼ to 4 hrs.
Tobermory	1¾ hrs.
Colonsay	2½ hrs.

STA.

ALBANY ST.

HIGH ST.

COMBIE ST.

A 816

—N—

0   ¼   ½ mile

LOCHGILPHEAD

STRANRAER

KIRKCOLM

A718

B737

VEHICLE FERRY TO
Larne	2¼ hrs.
Douglas	6 hrs.*
*(Summer only)	

LOCH RYAN

STA.

A77

GLENLUCE

A75

A77

PORTPATRICK

0   ½ mile

—N—

Legend to City Centre Maps (following pages)

ROAD INFORMATION	INFORMATION ROUTIERE	TOURIST INFORMATION	RENSEIGNEMENTS TOURISTIQUES	ABBREVIATIONS	ABREVIATIONS
Motorway	Autoroute	Important building	Edifice important	Cath — Cathedral	Cathédrale
(18) Junction number	Numéro d'échangeur	P Parking	Parking	Hospl — Hospital	Centre hospitalier
Main road	Route principale	Railway station	Gare	HPO — Head Post Office	Bureau de poste principal
Secondary road	Route secondaire	Underground/Metro station	Station de métro	Liby — Library	Bibliothèque
Pedestrian area	Zone piétonnière	Bus or coach station	Gare d'autobus ou d'autocar	Mus — Museum	Musée
		i Information Centre	Bureau de renseignements	NTS — National Trust for Scotland	National Trust d'Ecosse
		+ Church with tower or spire	Eglise avec tour ou flèche	TH — Town Hall	Hôtel de ville

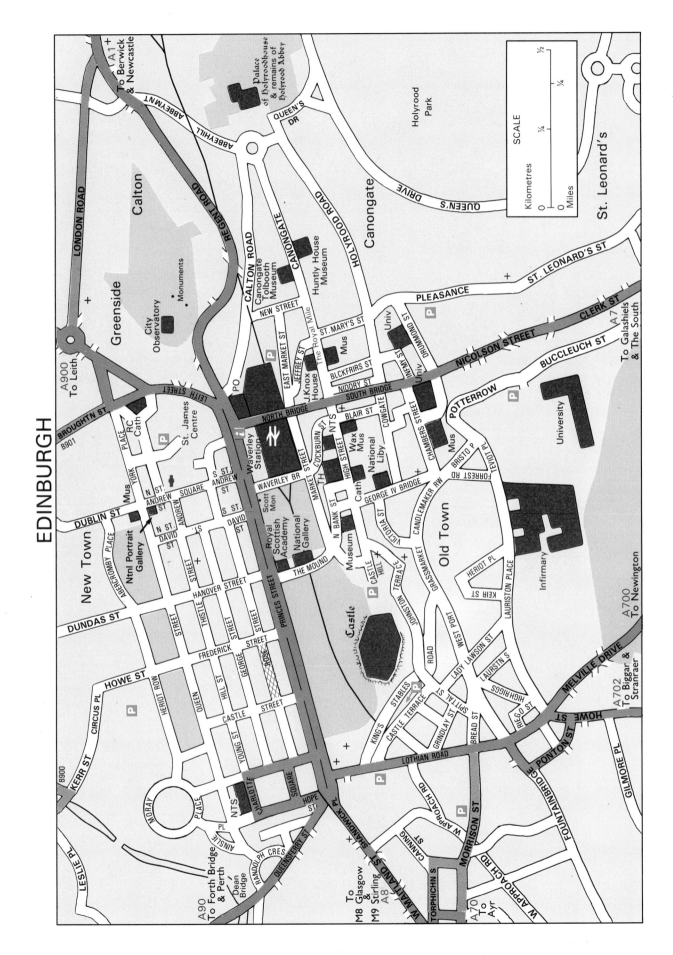

EDINBURGH

New Town

Old Town

Greenside

Calton

Canongate

Castle

St. Leonard's

Holyrood Park

Palace of Holyroodhouse & remains of Holyrood Abbey

City Observatory

Monuments

Canongate Tolbooth Museum

Huntly House Museum

J.Knox House

Wax Mus

National Liby

Cath

Museum

Scott Mon

Royal Scottish Academy

National Gallery

Ntnl Portrait Gallery

Mus

St. James Centre

RC Cath

Infirmary

University

SCALE

Kilometres

Miles

LONDON ROAD

REGENT ROAD

ABBEYHILL

ABBEYMNT

QUEEN'S DR

QUEEN'S DRIVE

CALTON ROAD

CANONGATE

HOLYROOD ROAD

Canongate

NEW STREET

ST. MARY'S ST

ST. LEONARD'S ST

PLEASANCE

CLERK ST

NICOLSON STREET

BUCCLEUCH ST

A7

To Galashiels & The South

POTTERROW

BRISTO P

FORREST RD

TEVIOT PL

BRISTO RD

CHAMBERS STREET

CANDLEMAKER RW

GEORGE IV BRIDGE

COWGATE

BLAIR ST

HIGH STREET

VICTORIA ST

GRASSMARKET

KEIR ST

HERIOT PL

LAURISTON PLACE

EAST MARKET ST

JEFFREY ST

BLCKFRIRS ST

NIDDRY ST

SOUTH BRIDGE

INFMY ST

DRUMMOND ST

Univ

Univ

Mus

NORTH BRIDGE

COCKBURN ST

MARKET STREET

WAVERLEY BR

THE MOUND

PRINCES STREET

Waverley Station

PO

N BANK ST

CASTLE HILL

JOHNSTON TERRACE

STABLES

KING'S

CASTLE TERRACE

SPITTAL ST

GRINDLAY ST

BREAD ST

WEST PORT

LADY LAWSON ST

LAURSTN S

HIGH RIGGS

RIEGO ST

PONTON ST

FOUNTAINBRIDGE

GILMORE PL

MELVILLE DRIVE

A700 To Newington

A702 To Biggar & Stranraer

HOWE ST

MORRISON ST

W APPROACH RD

CANNING ST

TORPHICHN S

W MAITLAND ST

SHANDWICK PL

QUEENSFERRY ST

RANDOLPH CRES

Dean Bridge

AINSLIE PL

MORAY PLACE

CHARLOTTE SQUARE

HOPE ST

NTS

PL

LESLIE PL

KERR ST

B900

CIRCUS PL

HERIOT ROW

DUNDAS ST

HOWE ST

HANOVER STREET

FREDERICK STREET

GEORGE STREET

CASTLE STREET

ROSE STREET

THISTLE STREET

HILL ST

YOUNG ST

QUEEN ST

ABERCROMBY PLACE

DUBLIN ST

BROUGHTN ST

B901

YORK PLACE

N ST

S ST

ANDREW ST

ANDREW SQUARE

DAVID ST

A900 To Leith

LEITH STREET

LOTHIAN ROAD

A90 To Forth Bridge & Perth

To M8 Glasgow & M9 Stirling A8

A70 To Ayr

A1 To Berwick & Newcastle

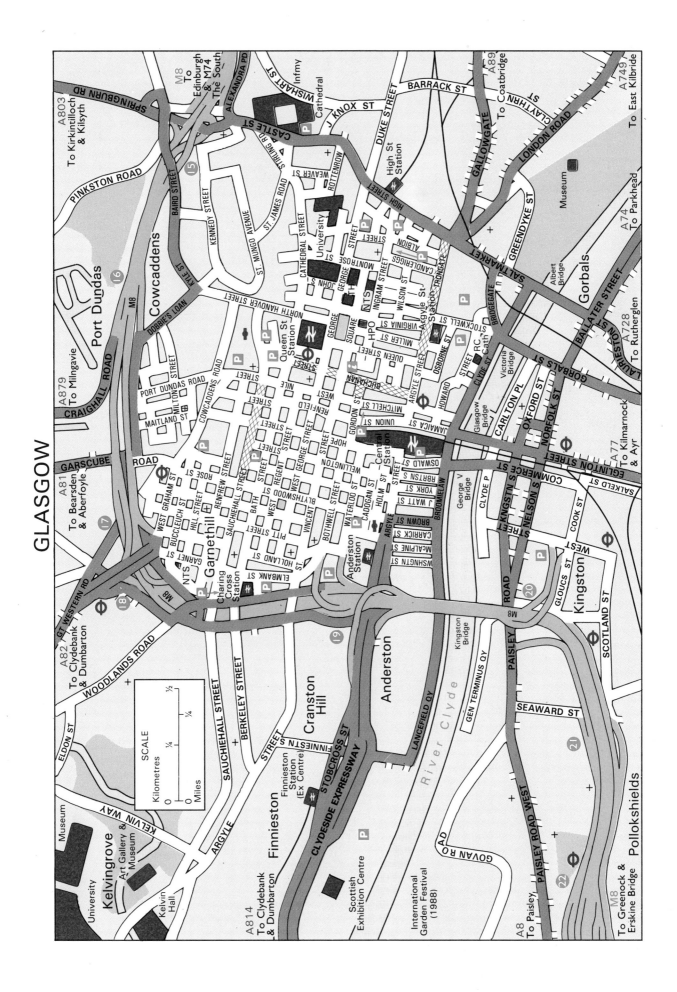

GLASGOW

M8 Port Glasgow – Coatbridge

Eastbound ▲   ▼ Westbound

A8 Greenock Bishopston
31
4
M898 Erskine Bridge **30** Erskine Bridge **M898**
3
A276 Paisley Bishopston / **A740** Linwood **29** Paisley **A726** / Linwood **A740**
1
Glasgow Airport **28** Glasgow Airport
1
A741 Renfrew Paisley **27** Renfrew **A741** Paisley
2
A8 Renfrew **A736** Hillington **26** Renfrew **(A8) A741** Hillington
1
A739 Clyde Tunnel No link with **A739** South **25** Clyde Tunnel **A739** No link with **A739** South
1
A77 Kilmarnock Govan **24** Irvine **A736**
1/2
23 Govan **B768**
1/2
22 Kilmarnock **M77** Prestwick Airport
1/2
A8 City Centre **A730** East Kilbride **21**
1/2
20 East Kilbride **A730** City Centre
1/2
A814 Clydebank **19**
Limited access **18** Charing Cross Limited access
A82 Dumbarton Limited access **17** Dumbarton **A82** Kelvinside Limited access
1/2
16 City Centre **A804** Aberfoyle **(A81)** Cowcaddens
1/2
A803 Kirkintilloch Townhead **15** City Centre **A8**
1
Fruit Market **14**
1
Carntyne **13** Dennistoun Fruit Market
1
A80 Stirling **12** Stirling **A80** Riddrie
1
B756 Garthamlock Queenslie **11** Garthamlock **B756** Queenslie
1
Easterhouse Barlanack **10** Easterhouse Barlanack
1
Easterhouse Bailliehouse **9**
1
M73 South, Carlisle / **A8** East, Edinburgh / **A89** East, Coatbridge **8** Access from **A8** and **A89** West, **M73** North
A8

M8 Airdrie – M9

Eastbound ▲   ▼ Westbound

6
6 Airdrie **A73** Lanark Motherwell **(A273)**
5
B7057 Shotts Harthill **5** Shotts **B7057** Harthill
2
Harthill Services ◇ Harthill Services
4
A801 Bathgate Whitburn Falkirk **4** Bathgate **A801** Whitburn Falkirk
6
A899 Livingston No link with **A899** Northbound **3** Livingstone **A899** No link with **A899** Northbound
6
A89 Broxburn / **A6** Edinburgh and Airport **2** Edinburgh and Airport **A8** Bathgate **A89**
2
M9

M9 Dunblane – M8

Northbound ▲   ▼ Southbound

A9 Perth Bridge of Allan **B824** Doune
11
3
A84 Callander Crianlarich Stirling **10** **(A9)** Stirling **A84**
4
A872 Stirling **9** **(A80)** Glasgow **M80** Carlisle Denny **A872** Falkirk
Services ◇ Services
5
M876 Glasgow **8**
1
M876 Kincardine Bridge **7** Kincardine Bridge **M876**
3
6 Grangemouth **A905** Falkirk
2
A905 Falkirk Grangemouth **5**
A801 Bathgate Livingston **A803** Polmont **4** Bathgate **A801** Livingston Linlithgow **A803** Kirkiston **B9080**
5
A803 Linlithgow Bo'Ness **3**
2
2 Uphill **B8046** Forth Road Bridge
4
A8000 Forth Road Bridge **1**
1
M8 Glasgow **A8** Edinburgh

M876 M80 – Kincardine Bridge

Eastbound ▲   ▼ Westbound

M80
2
A883 Falkirk Denny Bonnybridge **1** Falkirk **A883** Denny
1
2 Falkirk **A9** Larbert
2
M9 Stirling **M9 J8** **M9** Eastbound only
M9 Grangemouth Edinburgh Falkirk **M9 J7** Grangemouth **M9** Edinburgh
1
3 Airth **A905**
A876 Kincardine Br

M90 Perth – Forth Road Bridge

Northbound ▲   ▼ Southbound

A9 The North Stirling Inverness Perth
11
3
M85 The North East Dundee Forfar Aberdeen **A912** Perth **10** Dundee **M85** Forfar Aberdeen Braemar
2
A912 Bridge of Earn Newburgh **9** Bridge of Earn **A912** Glenfarg **(B996)** Cupar **(A913)**
9
A91 St Andrews Dundee Tay Bridge Glenfarg **8**
2
7 Milnathort **A91** Stirling
1
A922 Kinross Milnathort **A977** Kincardine Br **6** Kinross **A922** Kincardine Br **A977**
Kinross Services ◇ Kinross Services
3
B9097 Crook of Devon Glenrothes **5** Crook of Devon **B9097** Glenrothes
3
B914 Dollar **A909** Kelly **4** Kelly **A909** Cowdenbeath
4
A907 Dumfermline Cowdenbeath **3** Kirkcaldy **A92** Dunfermline **A907**
3
A823 Dunfermline **2** Rosyth **A823** Dunfermline
1
A921 Kirkcaldy **A985** Kincardine Br **1** Inverkeithing **A921** Kirkcaldy Kincardine Br **A985**
A90
Forth Road Bridge (toll)

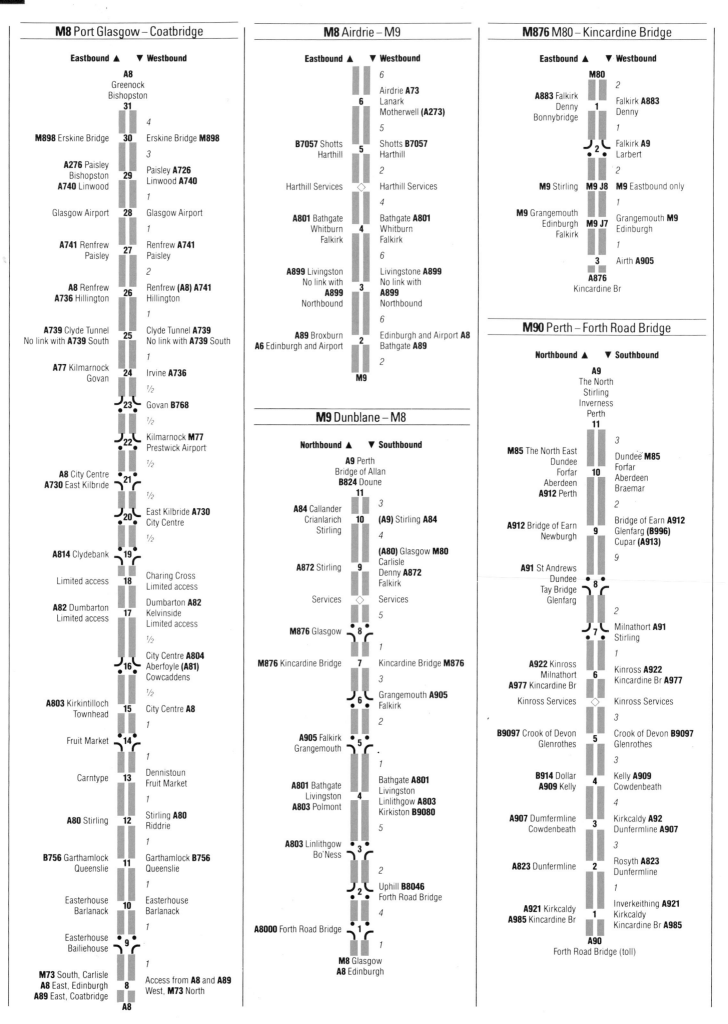

Motorways

Key

15 junction number

⌐ access or exit at a limited interchange

● no access or no exit at a limited interchange

3 intermediate distance in miles

◇ services

Index to 3 miles: 1 inch Maps

How to use this index

For each entry the Atlas page number is listed and an alpha-numeric map reference is given to the grid square in which the name appears. For example:

Aberdeen .... 103 G3.

Aberdeen will be found on page 103, square G3.

The National Grid

The blue grid lines which appear on the Atlas map pages are from the Ordnance Survey National Grid. The National Grid is a reference system which breaks the country down into squares to enable a unique reference to be given to a place or feature. This reference will always be the same no matter which Ordnance Survey map product is used. The squares which form the basic grid cover an area of 100 kilometres by 100 kilometres and are identified by letters; eg NG, NS. These squares are subdivided by grid lines each carrying a reference number. The numbering sequence runs East and North from the South West corner of Great Britain.

Grid lines on the Atlas map pages appear at 10 kilometre intervals. The 100 kilometre lines are shown in a darker blue. Those grid lines which fall at the top, bottom and outside edge of each page of Atlas mapping also carry their reference numbers (eg ^{2}4) printed in blue. The larger number is the reference of the actual grid line, the smaller that of the preceding 100 kilometre grid line. The letters which identify each 100 kilometre square appear on the Atlas mapping also printed in blue.

A leaflet on the National Grid referencing system is available from Information and Enquiries, Ordnance Survey, Romsey Road, Maybush, Southampton SO9 4DH.

Region and Island Area Names showing abbreviations used in this Index

Regions	
Borders	Border
Central	Central
Dumfries & Galloway	D. & G.
Fife	Fife
Grampian	Grampn
Highland	Highl
Lothian	Lothn
Strathclyde	Strath
Tayside	Tays

Island Areas	
Orkney	Orkney
Shetland	Shetld
Western Isles	W. Isles

Abbey St Bathans   Aultbea

A

Abbey St Bathans	77 G1	Achmore, Highld	107 H5
Aberargie	86 A1	Achnacarnin	124 D5
Aberchalder	99 F3	Achnacarry	98 D5
Aberchirder	112 D3	Achnacloich	97 E3
Aberdalgie	93 G6	Achnaconeran	99 G2
Aberdeen	103 G3	Achnacroish	90 C4
Aberdour	86 A4	Achnagarron	110 A1
Aberfeldy	93 E4	Achnahanat	120 B4
Aberfoyle	84 B2	Achnahannet	110 D6
Aberlady	86 D5	Achnairn	120 B2
Aberlemno	95 E3	Achnamara	82 B4
Abernethy	86 A1	Achnasaul	98 D5
Abernyte	94 B5	Achnasheen	108 D3
Aberuthven	85 F1	Achreamie	124 D2
Abington	75 F5	Achriesgill	122 D3
Aboyne	102 C4	Ackergill	125 G3
Abriachan	109 H5	Addiewell	75 F1
Abune-the-Hill	126 B2	Advie	111 F5
Achachork	106 D4	Ae	67 F4
Achahoish	82 B5	Affleck	103 F1
Achanalt	109 E2	Aignish	117 G4
Achandunie	110 A1	Aikerness	128 C3
Ach' an Todhair	98 C6	Aikers	126 D5
Achaphubuil	98 C6	Aird, Strath	82 B2
Acharacle	90 A2	Aird, D. & G.	64 C6
Acharn	92 D4	Aird, W. Isles	117 H4
Achath	102 E2	Aird Dell	117 G1
Achfary	122 D5	Aird Mhànais	115 F4
Achgarve	118 B6	Aird Mheadhonach	115 F3
Achiemore	124 B3	Aird of Sleat	97 E3
Achiltibuie	118 D3	Aird Riabhach	115 G3
Achina	123 J2	Airdrie	84 D6
Achinduich	120 B4	Airdriehill	85 D6
Achingills	125 E2	Aird, The	106 D3
Achintee	108 B4	Aird Thunga	117 G4
Achintraid	107 H5	Aird Uig	116 C4
Achleck	89 F3	Airntully	93 G5
Achluachrach	99 F5	Airor	97 G3
Achlyness	122 D3	Airth	85 E4
Achmelvich	118 D1	Aith, Shetld	131 E5
Achmore, W. Isles	117 F5	Aith, Orkney	127 F2
		Aithsetter	132 B4
		Alcaig	109 H3
		Aldclune	93 E2

Aldochlay	83 H3
Aldunie	111 H6
Alexandria	83 H4
Alford, Grampn	102 C2
Allanaquoich	101 F4
Allanton, Strath	75 E4
Allanton, Border	77 H2
Allardice	103 F6
Alligin Shuas	107 H3
Alloa	85 E3
Alloway	73 H6
Allt na h-Airbhe	119 E4
Allt-nan-Sugh	108 B6
Almondbank	93 G6
Alness	110 A2
Altandhu	118 C2
Altass	120 B3
Alterwall	125 F2
Altnaharra	123 G5
Altrua	98 E4
Alva	85 E3
Alves	111 F2
Alvie	100 C3
Alyth	94 B4
Amatnatua	120 A4
Amhuinnsuidhe	114 E2
Amisfield	67 G4
Amulree	93 F5
Anaheilt	90 C2
Anancaun	108 C2
An rd	107 H1
An Caol	107 F3
Anchachork	106 D4
Ancrum	77 F5
Ankerville	110 C1
Annan	68 A6
Annat, Highld	108 A3
Annat, Strath	91 E6
Annathill	84 D5
Annbank	74 A5
Annochie	113 G4
Anstruther	87 E2
Anwoth	61 G4
Appin	90 D4

Applecross	107 G4
Appletreehall	76 E6
Aquahorthies	113 F6
Aquhythie	102 E2
Arabella	120 E6
Arbirlot	95 F4
Arboll	121 E5
Arbroath	95 F4
Arbuthnott	103 F6
Archiestown	111 G4
Ardachu	120 C3
Ardalanish	89 E6
Ardanaiseig	91 E6
Ardaneaskan	107 H5
Ardarroch	107 H5
Ardbeg	80 D6
Ardcharnich	119 E5
Ardchiavaig	89 E6
Ardchyle	92 B6
Ard-dhubh	107 G4
Ardchive	98 D4
Ardelve	108 A6
Arden	83 H4
Ardentinny	83 F4
Ardeonaig	92 C5
Ardersier	110 B3
Ardessie	118 D5
Ardfern	82 C2
Ardgay	120 B4
Ardgowan	83 G5
Ardhasaig	115 F2
Ardheslaig	107 G3
Ardindrean	119 E5
Ardivachar	105 C5
Ardivachar Point	105 C5
Ardlair	112 C6
Ardler	94 B4
Ardlui	83 H1
Ardlussa	82 A4
Ardmair	119 E4
Ardminish	70 B2
Ardmolich	97 G6
Ardnacroish	90 C4

Ardnadam	83 F4
Ardnagrask	109 H4
Ardnarff	108 A5
Ardnastang	90 C2
Ardo	113 F5
Ardoyne	112 D6
Ardrishaig	82 C4
Ardroil	116 C4
Ardross	109 J1
Ardrossan	73 G3
Ardshealach	90 A2
Ardtalnaig	92 D5
Ardtoe	97 F6
Ardtornish	90 B4
Ardulie	109 H2
Ardvasar	97 F3
Ardvey, W. Isles	115 E4
Ardvey, W. Isles	115 F3
Ardvourlie	115 F1
Ardwell	60 C5
Aridhglas	89 E5
Arinacrinachd	107 G3
Arinagour	88 D2
Arisaig	97 F5
Arivruaich	117 E6
Armadale, Highld	124 A2
Armadale, Lothn	85 F6
Arncroach	86 E2
Arnisdale	97 H2
Arnish	107 E4
Arniston Engine	76 C1
Arnol	117 F3
Arnprior	84 C3
Arpafeelie	109 J3
Arrochar	83 G2
Artafallie	110 A4
Arthrath	113 G5
Ascog	73 F1
Ashfield, Central	85 D2
Ashgill	75 D3
Ashkirk	76 D5
Asknish	82 D3
Asloun	102 C2
Athelstaneford	87 E5

Attadale	108 B5
Auchagallon	72 C4
Aucharnie	112 D4
Auchattie	102 D4
Auchenblae	102 E6
Auchenbrack	66 D3
Auchencairn	62 B1
Auchencarroch	84 A4
Auchencrow	77 H1
Auchengray	75 F2
Auchenhalrig	111 H2
Auchenheath	75 E3
Auchentiber	73 H3
Auchgourish	100 D2
Auchindrain	83 E2
Auchindrean	119 E5
Auchininna	112 D4
Auchinleck	74 B5
Auchinloch	84 C5
Auchleuchries	113 H5
Auchleven	102 D1
Auchlochan	75 E4
Auchlossan	102 C3
Auchlyne	92 B6
Auchmillan	74 B5
Auchmithie	95 F4
Auchnacree	94 D2
Auchnagallin	111 E5
Auchnagatt	113 G4
Auchrerarder	85 F1
Auchteraw	99 F3
Auchterderran	86 B3
Auchtermuchty	86 B1
Auchterneed	109 G3
Auchtertool	86 B3
Auchtertyre	107 H6
Auchtubh	92 B6
Auckengill	125 G2
Auds	112 D2
Auldearn	110 D3
Auldhame	87 E4
Auldhouse	74 C2
Ault a' Chruinn	98 B1
Aultbea	118 B5